INSECURE
ATTACHMENT

Proven Steps For Overcoming Emotional Trauma, Codependency, Avoidant Attachment, and Fear of Abandonment | Therapy for Building Stronger Personal Relationships

LARA CARTER

Table Of Contents

"If an individual is capable of loving positively, he also loves himself; if he can only love others, he cannot love at all."

Erich Fromm, The art of loving

Preface

In recent years there has been a change in society linked to technological progress and a continuous increase in the need for material resources. In addition, high levels of image standards are emerging that make people increasingly insecure about themselves and their values. All this has led to the development of new pathological addictions that are still little considered, including emotional dependence. Affective dependence is a very common psychological condition, especially in women, but it can also be found in a small percentage of men. It lays the foundations already in childhood, in the education we receive from parents and in the relationship that is established with them from birth.

INTRODUCTION

Dependence is defined as "a condition, in which an individual finds himself, incoercibly in need of a product or a substance, especially drugs, alcohol, drugs, to which he has become accustomed, and whose abstinence can cause in him a state of depression, discomfort and anguish, and sometimes more or less violent physical disorders, ie nausea, widespread pain, contractions, etc..

"There is a healthy dependence and a pathological one, the first has as its object the things useful for our survival (oxygen, water, food, ...). The second can arise from the use of drugs and alcohol abuse as well as gambling, commonly considered addictions. Unfortunately, in recent years we are witnessing the emergence of new and little considered addictions as a result of daily behavior that provide us with small continuous gratifications as a "like" on a photo published on a social page.

Attention must be paid to the needs that risk becoming a source of dependence, such as food, especially in rich countries.

A form of pathological dependence that is still little known is affective dependence, a psychological condition that has been widespread especially in recent years, but underestimated or not considered because it does not manifest itself with specific symptoms and it is difficult to recognize it and become aware of it. It develops more in women, but can also be found in a small percentage of men. This type of dependence lays the foundations already in childhood, in fact from birth the child establishes models of emotional attachment that will condition his personality and the relationship with others. If the level of these early forms of relationships is not adequate, the child may develop unhealthy relationships as an adult. In addition, a pattern of dysfunctional attachment and childhood trauma can develop personality disorders. This risks developing a different way of seeing relationships and the person in front of you: because of the need to feel the closeness of the other person you delude yourself that the relationship is perfect, the person by your side seems to be the best, the only one that can really make us happy, but behind this appearance lies a dark side, made of psychological violence. And it is important to recognize this form of violence before it also moves physically. Affective dependence is a widespread phenomenon nowadays, as people feel increasingly insecure about their way of being because of the pressures generated by the increasingly high standards of image, and thus feel the need to be accepted and desired by someone even at the cost of suffering psychological and physical violence. Both destabilize the person inwardly causing serious problems both physically, such as anorexia and bulimia, and psychologically, such as psychosis, personality disorders, schizophrenia, mood disorders. Often physical violence seems to us to be something very far from our daily reality, but unfortunately it is much closer than you can imagine as we are told by a statistic that comes from the United States in which one in three women has suffered physical violence from intimate partner. This form of violence has taken on such importance that it has been defined by the WHO as Intimate Partner Violence (IPV) and is associated with various alterations in physical health conditions, somatic symptoms and unhealthy behaviour. IPV can take the form of verbal assaults or threats, physical attacks, sexual violence or coercion.

CHAPTER 1

THE ORIGINS OF EMOTIONAL DEPENDENCE

To better understand the mechanisms underlying this problem, it is necessary to analyze the thoughts and theories of various psychologists in relation to the process of development of the child and the parental role in education.

The first psychoanalyst I would like to mention is Freud, who has studied the personality of the individual and emotional development a lot. It divides the latter into five phases, during which the relationship established between parents and children and the satisfaction of desires that characterize each phase is important.

In addition, he deepens the phase of the Oedipus complex whose resolution is important for the formation of the personality and the development of healthy intimate relationships. Erikson expands the Freudian theory by identifying eight phases of psychosocial development, each of which is characterized by a crisis, seen in a positive sense, important for the construction of one's own identity.

For the development of this, he gives importance, in addition to the relationship that is established with parents, the environment around him and the society in which the individual lives.

Starting from classical psychoanalytic theories, in particular that of Freud, Melanie Klein and other psychoanalysts, they develop the theory of object relations that places great importance on the relationship that is established between the mother and the child since intrauterine life.

But in order to better understand the processes through which an individual gains his autonomy, it is necessary to introduce the concept of attachment. Both attachment and dependence have in common a bond with another person, but usually attachment does not prevent detachment, while dependence does. The attachment theory was formulated by Bowlby which identifies three attachment styles with the mother that the child can develop in the first years of life and that will affect her whole life.

Mary Ainsworth expands her theory by studying the bonds of attachment in adults through a diagnostic, research and observation tool of the mother-child relationship, called "strange situation".

In this chapter I will analyze how the bond of attachment that is established will condition the individual and his relationships.

Freud's Theories

As mentioned previously, the psychoanalyst Freud explores the theme of the development of affectivity in children. He introduces new techniques such as dream analysis and free associations with the aim of bringing past events back to consciousness. In fact, he says that what we experienced as children will affect our personality.

Moreover, he argues that man's behaviour is dictated by pleasure, by the search for fulfillment and by the realization of one's desires. However, this desire clashes with reality, with rules and difficulties, and from this clash arise frustrations. When the individual follows pleasure and his own desires he adopts a primary process, when he renounces it and follows reality, he adopts a secondary process.

According to his theory, development is seen as the transition from the primary process to the secondary process based primarily on logic.

Freud divides the personality of the individual into three components: Me, Es and Super Me. The Ego follows the principle of reality and allows the subject to differentiate between internal and external reality. The totally unconscious Es, on the other hand, follows its own desires and therefore pleasure. Finally, the Super I is born from the internalization of the norms imposed by society or by parents and has the objective of strengthening the ego when it follows these norms or, on the contrary, weakening it when it does not follow them, thus producing anxiety and guilt. According to Freud, affective development develops through stages: the oral phase (0-18 months), the anal phase (18 months-3 years), the phallic phase (3 years-5 years), the latency phase (from 6 years to puberty) and the adult genital phase (from puberty). Each stage is linked to a part of the body that will become the half of the drive. However, they do not have a rigid configuration, but it is possible to move on to the next step even without having passed the previous one. When, however, the impulse of each phase is not completely satisfied, or, on the contrary, is satisfied too much, a "fixation" can develop, thus preventing the subject from moving to the next phase. This can be related to childhood trauma or the inability of the subject to leave the phase where he has found more satisfaction.

Often the obsessions, when they are healthy, manifest themselves with trivial and unconscious gestures such as constantly touching one's hair or eating one's nails. However, when they become pathological, the person consciously organizes his or her life around certain behaviours, putting in the background more important aspects of life such as work and one's own relationships, and when he or she cannot put them into practice, he or she will feel a sense of unease.

In this case the person can develop obsessive-compulsive pathologies. Some of the adult behaviors may result from a regression or from residues of the stages of affective development.

For example, a regression of the oral phase can lead the subject to passive-dependent behaviour, protective attitudes towards others and pessimistic attitudes.

Aggression and dominance, on the other hand, are personality traits linked to the phallic phase.

If, on the other hand, the child is unable to overcome the phases of child sexuality, there could be neurotic behaviour or sexual perversions.

Therefore, overcoming the Oedipus complex plays an important role in achieving a mature sexuality, fundamental for a balanced social life.

The Oedipus complex represents a normal phase of the child's emotional development that Freud places within the phallic phase, linked to sexual identity. Freud uses the term for both sexes, however Jung introduces for girls the term complex of Elettra, but with the same mode of development. The Oedipus complex consists of the competition that the child has for the parent of his or her own sex, due to the attraction for the parent of the opposite sex. Therefore, the child will become possessive towards the mother figure and will be altered if the father expresses affectionate gestures towards the mother. In the same way it happens in the girls towards the father figure. Usually the Oedipus complex resolves spontaneously with the progressive identification with the parent of one's own sex.

Between the ages of three and five, the child understands, through his father's calls, that he cannot satisfy his instincts and will manifest such anger: this is the phase of the castration complex.

Finally, at around the age of five-six, the child, for fear of being punished, will gradually give up taking the place of the parent of his or her own sex and will shift his or her attention to another person of the opposite sex outside the family.

The way in which the Oedipus complex is approached and overcome depends on the previous phases and on the relationship that parents create with their children. Failure to overcome this phase would be at the origin of most of the psychic disorders and the birth of problematic relationships. In addition, in the event that the child lacks a father figure, the child will identify with the mother and as a result may, as an adult, be interested in persons of the same sex. As if the parent were to refuse the child's affection, he or she might develop a sense of guilt and shame that will cause him or her difficulties in establishing healthy intimate relationships.

The Theories Of Erikson

While Freud's emotional development took place in five phases, psychologist and psychoanalyst Erikson identifies eight stages of psychosocial development, as it also takes into account the third age.

Each stage is characterized by a crisis due to the conflict between two opposing tendencies:

1. 1 Confidence/faith phase, 0-1 year (Freudian oral phase): the child needs to be fed and cared for and the satisfaction of his primary needs creates in him a feeling of trust in the world. In this phase, the relationship established with the mother is very important.
   If the relationship is disturbed, the child will feel a sense of distrust that will extend to the reality around him.
2. Autonomy/shame and doubt phase, 1-3 years (Freudian anal phase): the child begins to differentiate the self from the not self; the sense of autonomy is born because the child begins to detach himself from the mother to explore the environment, but if he feels frustrated or mocked feelings of shame and doubt arise.
   Moreover, if the parents are too anxious and hinder their psychomotricity, the child will freeze and will not be able to obtain their autonomy, but rather will see it in a negative sense as a source of frustration and become insecure in their behavior by developing doubts about their skills.
3. Phase of initiative/fault, 3-6 years (Freudian genital/oedipal phase): the child begins to develop a sense of morality and duty. If the phase is not resolved in the best possible way, by increasing and directing the spirit of initiative, or by accepting the child's new curiosities, a strong sense of guilt will be born in the child.
4. Phase of industriousness/inferiority, 6-12 years (Freudian latency phase): the child needs to obtain the approval of others, both at school from teachers and in social relations.
   On the contrary, if this does not happen, a sense of inferiority will arise in him.
5. Phase of identity, 12-20 years (Freudian genital phase): the individual tries to build his own identity on the basis of the Ego that has been built up to now in relation to the other various models with which he is confronted.
   In this phase the role of the parents and the way they relate to the adolescent is important: they should not adopt ambiguous or confusing behaviors but adapt to its normal changes related to the hormonal storm. An inadequate development of identity can lead to the development of psychosis or psychopathy.
6. Phase of intimacy and isolation, 20-40 years old: the young man wants to compare his built identity with others and thus begins

to build intimate relationships, both loving and friendly. If, on the other hand, the construction of the identity has not been completed, the individual will be afraid of a complete and demanding relationship and will tend to isolate himself.

7. Generativity/stagnation phase, 40-65 years: the individual feels the need to create and generate something useful, at work and in the family, to pass on to the next generations.
    This is the goal that the person sets himself in this period that, if not achieved, will give rise in her a sense of stagnation and uselessness referred to his existence.

8. Phase of the integrity of the I/desperation, from 65 onwards: phase of old age in which the elderly person reflects on himself/herself, on what he/she has done in his/her life and on the mistakes he/she has made. If he has achieved a good feeling of integrity and completeness, he will not be afraid of death but will face it calmly.

Erikson argues that each stage is built on the basis of the previous ones and will influence the subsequent ones.

If the crises of each phase are not overcome, the individual will continue to fight to resolve them even in adulthood.

The resolution of these crises is fundamental to the construction of one's own identity, the most difficult and important objective in the life of every individual.

According to Erikson's theory, therefore, parents play a very important role in building their own identity which, in turn, is important in building healthy intimate relationships.

The mother plays an important role from the beginning, if there is already a lack of confidence in oneself and in the world, it will be difficult for the individual to realize himself, build a good identity and live peacefully intimate relationships.

Just as the presence of parents who are too anxious to hinder the child's autonomy may give rise to a need for continuous parenthood in him, first by the parents and then by the chosen partner, who in turn will be an individual with other problems always related to his emotional development.

Moreover, while for Freud each phase of emotional development is linked to a part of the body, Erikson gives great importance to the social environment in which the child lives and, consequently, how it influences the personal growth of the person, the resolution of crises that characterize each phase and, therefore, the construction of their own identity.

Theories Of Object Relations

The theories of object relations are based on the principle that the individual has an innate tendency to relate to others from birth, indeed already during intrauterine life has established a relationship with the mother that will tend to seek during the early stages of development, for the satisfaction of its needs and its survival, and that will affect future relationships.

The term "object relation" refers to motivational, cognitive and affective processes related to the ability to build and maintain intimate relationships with other people (Western, 1998).

The newborn baby gradually begins to perceive the presence of the people around him, and then to internalize the "objects" by establishing relationships with them. The object is the reference figure that is usually the mother. Fairbairn argues that the development of object relations is a process through which child dependence on the object gradually gives way to a mature dependence on the object.

Many authors have dealt with the theory of object relations.

Ronald Fairbairn focuses on the relationship between mother and child, which is important for healthy development.

He argues that the child is oriented from birth to enter into a relationship with others, because what he is looking for is direct contact with others and not body pleasure. Pleasure is only the means to achieve relationship with each other.

Therefore, it departs from Freud's theory that gave more importance to the search for pleasure and to the satisfaction of one's own impulses and set pleasure as a goal. Winnicott also focuses on the mother-child relationship, without which we could not speak of the psycho-social development of the child.

The individual has an innate tendency to relate to others and through the internalization of these relationships will form intrapsychic structures called Bowlby's internal operating models, which I will explore later. The psychoanalyst who has dealt most with object relations is Melanie Klein. According to Klein, the impulse is linked to the object, because the child has a deep relationship with reality and everything around him.

The goal of the impulse is pleasure and the object is only a means to achieve this goal.

In this respect, Klein approaches Freud's theory and departs from Fairbairn's. He also argues that the way in which the internal and external worlds relate depends on how the external experiences are represented internally. Internal and external experiences greatly influence psychic development. The theorists of object relations argue that the psychic structure is constituted by "internalized object relations". The development of the personality derives from the relationship that the child has had with his own object: if he has had a good relationship he will have a stable and serene personality; on the contrary, if the object has been unreliable or unavailable the child will be able to develop an unstable and pathological personality. Therefore, the relationship with the mother figure is very important since the intrauterine life, because it will be on the basis of this that all future relationships, expectations about these and the personality of the individual will develop.

The failure of this relationship involves a risk for the development of permanent psychic alterations in adulthood, psychosomatic disorders and abnormalities in the psychomotor, cognitive, affective and relational development of the child.

From The Imprinting Of Lorenz To The Attachment Of Bowlbys

The ethologist Konrad Lorenz, following an experiment on wild geese, elaborated the concept of "imprinting". This means a form of early learning in which newborns at birth are attracted to the first person they see and develop a particular attachment to him that will affect his whole life.

He defines it as the fixation of a precise behavioural model that will be stable and irreversible. Lorenz's imprinting theory lays the foundation for the development of Bowlby's attachment theory.

He believes that the attachment bond develops through phases. In the first eight to twelve weeks of life the child is not able to discriminate against people, but he can recognize the mother by her voice and smell.

Gradually he will begin to distinguish the people who come into contact with him until, about the ninth month, he will arrive at a visible and stable attachment to the reference figure that is used as a basis for exploring the environment, always seeking protection and support.

This bond remains stable until about three years, when the child will feel calm even in unknown environments with the certainty that his reference figure will always return to him.

Therefore, it is in this period that the bond of attachment with the mother develops. Bowlby believes that attachment will be safe if the child receives affection and a sense of protection in the right measure from the bond with the reference figure, on the contrary it will be insecure if there is excessive prudence, dependence and instability.

He introduces the concept of "safe basis" by referring to the importance of the bond with the mother, who has the task of providing the child with a safe basis from which he can move away to make new acquaintances and return to receive comfort and security.

Bowlby identifies in particular three types of attachment:

- the safe attachment in which the mother is attentive to the needs of the child, but at the same time leaves him free to explore the world and guarantees his presence when he returns to her.

When this child becomes an adult, he or she will have a good self-esteem which he or she will maintain even in the most difficult situations and will establish good social relations.

- ambivalent attachment develops when the mother is and is not there, or alternates, often unconsciously, moments of maximum presence to others of absence. The child will thus become an adult with low self-esteem, insecure and with a constant fear of being abandoned.
- Avoiding attachment develops when the mother only provides the child with basic needs and not with emotional needs such as the need for security and belonging. The child learns to manage his own emotions and as an adult in relationships will appear detached and uncomfortable in physical and emotional intimacy.

Bowlby supports the importance of establishing an appropriate bond of attachment with the child, which will then be internalized by him and for this reason will affect his personality, his actions and his future relationships.

Among these models, what we are most interested in examining is the ambivalent style, as it is the one developed by affective employees. The constant fear they felt as children of losing their reference figure will reoccur in every relationship they establish. They will therefore have insane relationships characterized by an obsessive involvement determined by a strong anxiety and fear of losing their often idealized partner. And they will be ready to suffer psychological or physical violence at the cost of not breaking the pathological link.

Mary Ainsworth investigates the type of bond between mother and child through the "strange situation": an experiment in which she places the child in a room and observes his behavior when the mother leaves him with a stranger and then returns.

From this it identifies three types of attachment: safe, ambivalent insecure and avoiding insecure; later it will also identify the disorganized style.

In the first case, the child completely relies on the mother (or the reference figure) both in normal and dangerous conditions, feeling free to explore the world without fearing its abandonment. In the insecure attachment avoiding the child is convinced that at the time of need will have no one to help him and, indeed, will be rejected. In this way, he will begin to gain experience, always seeking autonomy also on an emotional level, where he will not express his feelings in order to avoid negative responses. The child does not cry at the moment of detachment from the mother and tends to avoid her at the moment of reunification. This comes from a mother who constantly rejects her son whenever he seeks attention or comfort. In the ambivalent insecure attachment the child does not have the certainty of being helped at the time of need, so in the exploration of the world will always be anxious and anxious for fear of abandonment.

This comes from a mother who is not always available to her child's requests and who even uses threats of abandonment as a means of coercion. Subsequently, it emerged that some children showed behaviours that could not be traced back to any of these types of attachment.

This is how we define the disoriented/disorganised style in which the child shows disorganised, incoherent, stereotyped behaviour, probably linked to a reference figure that arouses fear. Starting from the strange situation, Main and Goldwyn wanted to deepen the childhood experiences and the type of attachment of the parents of the children subjected to the experiment. The method used is the "Adult Attachment Interview" (A.A.I.): it is a semi-structured interview, formed by 15 questions aimed at remembering childhood, bringing unconscious feelings to consciousness and investigating internal operating models. The first questions are aimed at getting to know the family context.

The subject is then asked to give five adjectives to the mother and father and to motivate them with examples to try to better understand the relationship with them.

With these questions we will try to understand which parent the subject was most attached to, how he experienced the first separation from them and how is the current relationship. The structure of the interview puts the subject at risk of contradicting himself. Moreover, in this way he reconstructs the past in the light of current experiences.

Through the various interviews Main and Goldwyn have identified three types of adult subjects:

- Autonomous or safe adults are those who have answered the questions consistently and appropriately, even if they have had a difficult past. They attach great importance to bonds of attachment and childhood experiences as they are very aware of their own experience with parents during childhood and the effect it has had.
- Spaced adults are those who describe parents in very positive terms, but in a general way without reporting specific memories. However, in the course of the interview they often contradict each other and do not give due importance to the experiences of childhood relationships, indeed they minimize them.
- Finally, concerned adults are those who describe the relationship with their parents in an irrelevant and unclear way. They are confused, with a passive and often angry attitude towards their attachment figure. This shows that these subjects are still emotionally involved by past experiences.

Therefore, one might think that the distanced and worried subjects had an attachment of an insecure type. There has been a correlation between the strange situation and the Adult Attachment Interview: autonomous mothers will have safe children, distant mothers will have avoiding children, worried mothers will have resistant children.

When the disorganized style was introduced in the strange situation, it was associated with another type of adult defined as unresolved disorganized.

The latter is a person who has suffered trauma during childhood, such as loss of a parent or abuse, and has not yet overcome them.

With these interviews we try to investigate not so much the type of attachment that adults have had with their parents, but more the childhood and the experiences lived and how these affect their relationship with their children.

However, I do not believe that there really is a linear transmission in the style of attachment. There is no doubt that childhood greatly influences the personality of each person and therefore the relationship that is established with the children, but there are many other components, such as the surrounding environment, which will greatly influence the growth of the child and his personality.

The Narcissism

Often the person who tends to manipulate the other with psychological violence in the relationship is a person suffering from a personality disorder called "narcissism".

The psychoanalyst Rubin argues that the narcissist is the one who believes he is the whole world. In fact, the narcissist is the one who tends to have control and manipulate others without putting himself in the shoes of the other.

They are individuals who think only of themselves, without humanity and a sense of empathy.

But behind this grandeur there are actually feelings of inferiority accompanied by uncertainty and dissatisfaction with themselves that lead them to continually seek admiration and approval from others.

Narcissists separate the self from the self, idealizing their own image and losing sight of the real one, which is unacceptable to them. Narcissism is both a psychological and a cultural condition. At the cultural level, it indicates a loss of values because there is a lack of empathy, sensitivity, interest in one's fellow human beings and their feelings.

This is linked precisely to the change in society that leads us to be more and more in competition with each other both in work and in relationships, and to appreciate and give much more value to material things than gestures of kindness or love.

Psychologically, narcissism describes a personality disorder characterized by an attitude of superiority over others linked to an excessive investment in one's image at the expense of oneself and one's being. Narcissists end up identifying themselves with the idealized image of themselves, because their real image of themselves is unacceptable to them.

The concept of narcissism was born in the eighties thanks to the theoretical contributions of Kohut and Kernberg.

Kernberg argues that there are three types of narcissism:

- healthy narcissism, which is characteristic of all individuals, is what leads us to be ambitious, motivated and achieve our life projects. It also leads to healthy interpersonal relationships;
- pathological narcissism, a real personality disorder characterized by an excessive investment of one's own image that is idealized, to the detriment of the real image of oneself.

According to Kernberg, narcissism develops in early childhood and is linked to pathological object relations characterized by a lack of empathy, and identifies a certain affinity with Borderline personality disorder.

Kohut, on the other hand, attaches greater importance to the failure of empathic responses by parental figures, which is why the Self is blocked in the course of its normal development. Several authors have tried to understand the origin and causes of the disorder.

In the field of psychoanalysis it has been seen that narcissism appears in subjects whose parents have ambitious expectations of them, but are at the same time hypercritical in the activities they perform. Or he can appear where his parents are already narcissistic. The concept of narcissistic personality disorder was formulated by Kohut who later introduced it in the Diagnostical and Statistic Manual of Mental Disorders (DSM). Already DSM IV included narcissistic personality disorder along with Borderline personality disorder in group B.

The diagnostic criteria are:

- a great sense of himself and of his own importance;
- unlimited fantasies of success, power, charm and beauty;
- he believes he is special and unique and that he has to attend and be understood only by other special people of high class;
- he requires excessive and constant admiration;
- he has the feeling that everything is due to him;
- he takes advantage of others to achieve his goals;
- he lacks empathy: is not able to recognize or identify with the feelings and needs of others;

- is often envious of others or believes that others envy him;
- shows arrogant and presumptuous behaviour or attitudes.

To diagnose a narcissistic personality disorder, at least five of these behaviours must be present. The disorder would develop in subjects where fears, failures or addictions have been met with criticism, rejection and abandonment during childhood.

People with this disorder treat others as if they were objects to be used to meet their own needs and then leave them, after a short time, unaware of their feelings. This is because of the fear that the great image of oneself will be invalidated. At the same time, the narcissist clashes with his feelings of inferiority and a deep sense of loneliness that lead him to have on the one hand an excessive and constant need to be reassured and loved, on the other hand a deep feeling of envy towards others.

So, the other will be his savior but at the same time a rival and the relationship with others will always tend to exploitation to increase their self-esteem.

When aggression is added to the patient's feeling of grandeur, what is called "malignant narcissism" develops, that is, besides feeling unique and special, he will feel omnipotent, capable of doing anything, feeling joy and satisfaction in inflicting pain and fear on others. All of us have our own image of how we are and we always try to have good self-esteem and a good perception of our own image. But narcissists differ precisely in the grandeur and omnipotence that they believe they have. They unconsciously behave like real egoists, cold and without feelings for others. However, they are very suffering people, behind this apparent image that they give of themselves hide a social uneasiness, a sense of loneliness and the important relational and affective difficulties that lead them to establish continuous anomalous relationships, of short duration and poor quality, to increase the grandeur of their image. In addition, this continuing need to be admired and the inability to accept criticism can lead to the development of a depressive disorder, eating disorders, such as anorexia nervosa, and substance use/abuse.

Yet, it is precisely the narcissists who tend to affective manipulation because even in affective relationships they try to manipulate the partner on the basis of their desires, regardless of the feelings of others, only for the continuous need to receive confirmations and increase their self-esteem. According to the data reported by the American Psychiatric Association (APA) the narcissistic disturb of personality is diagnosed mainly in male adults while in females is found mostly Borderline personality disorder.

Emotional Dependence

If in the previous chapter I dealt with the theme of narcissism, therefore the point of view of the affective manipulator, we now see the affective dependence, that is the psychological condition that characterizes the victim. In addictions the subject is totally absorbed by the object of his own addiction, to the point of not being able to do without it, thus neglecting his life both at work and in relationships.

Therefore, it is a problem that has many physical and psychic consequences.

Dependence is not so much linked to the object on which one depends as to the relationship that is established between the subject and the object and the context in which both are inserted. It is difficult to give a definition of emotional dependence precisely because it is a very complex condition that involves many aspects of the individual. Personality disorders also include "personality dependent disorder". Affective dependence can be defined as "a relational mode in which a subject continually turns to others for help, guidance and support. The dependent individual, having little confidence in himself, bases his self-esteem on reassurance, on the approval of others and is unable to make decisions without external encouragement". It is argued that what comes from an event reacts on the causes, going to restructure the experience and the perception of oneself. Therefore, it is not the causes that provoke the behaviour, but the outcome of the behaviour itself that, becoming particularly significant for that subject, will facilitate its repetition. From this theory it is possible to formulate a definition of emotional dependence stating that it is "what results from the intersection between the power that the substance has and the power that the person is willing to attribute to the substance". The subject with a certain history, certain personal characteristics and a series of needs, when he meets the object that can be a substance, a behavior or a relationship, lives a restructuring of the self for which he becomes dependent. Schaffer (1964) argues that the basis of dependence is subjective experience, i.e. the way in which the object changes the condition of the individual. According to this vision, therefore, addiction is not a vice or a disease, but a process that is triggered when a person, when he comes into contact with a particular object, experiences new sensations that he interprets as more positive and functional. It is the individual's conviction that he has found a place to satisfy his essential needs and desires, which otherwise would not be possible to satisfy, according to his vision. Dependence, therefore, is not determined by specific causes, but by specific needs that derive from the needs of children who have remained unfulfilled. For example, a child growing up with a cold and unaffected parent may, as an adult, have emotional and relational problems and choose partners who are not affectively available. This is because as adults we tend to find people with whom we can have the same role that we had as children. Repeating the attachment pattern of childhood is easier than creating a new and healthier one. American Robin Norwood argues that "a healthier man who really loves us cannot play an important role in our lives until we have learned to free ourselves from the need to relive the old struggle again and again. Numerous studies have been carried out on the relationship between child attachment and emotional dependence. The results show that dependent subjects come from families where parents are overprotective or authoritarian. It is also true, however, that in some cases the opposite happens: when you grow up with parents who are too apprehensive you look for a relationship in which you feel free and autonomous.

Moreover, it has been seen that girls who have a conflicting relationship with their father are more likely to establish affective relationships pathological, than those who have had a peaceful relationship with him.

They are emotionally fragile women who need constant confirmation precisely to compensate for those they have never obtained before.

The only difference is that the first one develops towards a person: the subject devotes all his physical and mental energies to the other on whom he depends. In fact, it is considered a pathological form of love: it develops more in women who see in love the resolution of their problems that often have deep roots as emotional gaps in childhood. They are therefore fragile people, constantly looking for a love that gratifies them, gives them affection and self-esteem that otherwise they do not have. They are subjects who seek attention and continuous confirmation to feel safe and strong, contrasting the discomfort and emotional emptiness that they perceive. In this condition of dependence they will begin to lose their spaces of independence, they will show disinterest in everything that does not concern the object of love and they will close in the relationship as a couple obsessed with the idea of losing the partner. Affective employees cannot fully enjoy love and relationships, but seek immediate pleasure and the overcoming of an insecurity that is so fulfilling and liberating once reached, that you then want to relive it all. Dependent people are not able to get out of this relationship, even if they claim that it is itself unsatisfactory, humiliating and often self-destructive because it also develops a real symptomatology such as generalized anxiety, depression, insomnia, lack of appetite, melancholy, obsessive ideas. The particularity of this addiction is that it can often not be diagnosed and the subject himself is not aware of it and may never be for the rest of his life. However, this problem will feed the onset of other serious psychological, physical and relational problems. Today, emotional dependence is also called love addiction, where we mean by addiction the general condition in which psychological dependence pushes the continuous search for the object without which existence becomes meaningless. Many studies carried out on this subject show that the relationship with the additive object can have sedative properties, alleviating moral suffering and physical pain. Giddens argues that addiction is characterized by drunkenness and dose. A bewilderment is the feeling that the employee has from the relationship and that it is essential for him to feel good. The dose, on the other hand, is the amount of time together with the partner that the employee is looking for and which is increasing more and more because of his constant need for continuous and concrete manifestations of affection. It is possible to free oneself from emotional dependence, but it is necessary to find a certain inner stability. You don't have to be constantly looking for a partner to fill a void that you feel inside, otherwise you would end up finding a person who makes us feel even more empty inside. A good level of self-esteem is needed in order to establish a healthy relationship and convince oneself, therefore, that it is not necessary to do everything to change the other person, but to change oneself and always put one's happiness first.

Psychological And Physical Violence

Very often, affective employees find themselves in relationships where they suffer intimate partner violence (IPV), understood as psychological, physical or sexual violence. Despite this, employees cannot get rid of this relationship, but live in the hope that one day the partner can change because they are convinced that their love can bring about a positive change in the other person.

Psychological IPV includes abuse, emotional and verbal strategies to arouse fear, belittle women's self-esteem, isolate them from relationships and control their activities.

Psychological VTE is very frequent and has many harmful effects on the psychological well-being of women. Many times women who are in this condition are more exposed to adopt behaviors at sexual risk, thus increasing the likelihood of contracting HIV and other sexually transmitted diseases. Numerous studies have found associations between IPV and the physical and mental health of those who suffer it. In particular, it has been shown that only psychological violence, without physical and sexual violence, increases the frequency of non migraine headaches, depression, post-traumatic stress disorder, anxiety, insomnia, chronic pain and alcohol and smoking abuse. When women are subjected to sexual violence, along with psychological and physical violence, there is a worsening of their mental health and it was seen that low self-esteem, depression and anxiety were associated with violence suffered by their intimate partner or a known attacker.

The results of the association between sexual IPV and negative health outcomes led researchers to assume that sexual violence, particularly when inflicted by intimate partners, has a unique and significant impact on the victim and can be particularly traumatizing. Some studies show the diagnosis of depression, bipolar disorder, anxiety, chronic pain and frequent headaches among those who suffer from BPH. In addition, a study was carried out on IPV in pregnant women. From this it emerged that psychological violence is the most common form of violence in pregnant women, thus increasing all the symptoms related to their condition and that they can cause further effects on the child. There are still few studies, however, regarding the experience of abused men. This theme is considered marginal or often non-existent. However, it would be good to consider this aspect too, given the existence of the problem. Some studies, based on experiences reported by men, show that the main cause of violence by women is the need for control related to their own insecurity and extreme jealousy. They are often women with a borderline personality disorder who can't control their anger and, in order not to be alone, prefer to have a "weak" man at their side to be able to manage at will. The use of force or deception to obtain sexual intercourse has not been reported, but subsequent studies have shown that some women have a tendency to lie about their use of contraception and abuse pregnancies to obtain commitment or return together with the man who had left them. Initially, the woman presented herself as "weak", inspiring trust and feelings of protection towards the man. Shortly afterwards a possessive character emerged, an excessive control of all its activities, thus transforming the relationship into a closed and exclusive relationship. It was also seen that the beginning of psychological violence was between marriage, or the beginning of cohabitation, and the birth of the first child, as the latter was seen as a threat to their exclusive relationship, since the attention of man shifted to the child. However, men suffered violence until it was also directed at children or when they discovered an extramarital relationship. Some of the reasons for this violence may be linked to a difficult family situation, such as early trauma or violent behaviour in the family, or to inadequate support from institutions that has allowed the woman to misuse the measures available to women who are really victims of abuse. Despite this, all men reported great difficulties in realizing their status as victims, so much so that their relationships lasted in some cases up to 20-25 years before they were able to act. They were often subjected to psychological violence in the form of threats and pressures on the economic side, so they felt obliged to support the family, but when the violence shifted to their children or the extramarital relationship was discovered these men could find the strength to act. Strong feelings of isolation, helplessness and emotional suffering have emerged from men in this condition. When they found themselves isolated from friends and relatives they asked for help from professionals, but without success. Some have been laughed at or not believed. This increases their sense of loneliness, malaise and discomfort. In fact, despite the fact that the conception of violence is changing, the male victim still remains a "taboo" in Western societies because of the belief that a man cannot be defeated by a woman, and that the woman cannot have traits of aggression, usually attributed to the man. Because of this conception of domestic violence in our societies, men tend to be marginalised and questioned. Moreover, the fear of being separated from their children or being mistaken for the attackers can prevent them from seeking help. And this is how they fail to meet their needs for care, health care and social care, and as a result their exposure to violence and that of their children is prolonged.

CHAPTER 2

HOW TO DEAL WITH EMOTIONAL DEPENDENCE: SELF-HELP GROUPS

It is very difficult to realize that you are in an insane relationship or, even more, that you have an emotional dependence. We always try to justify the pathological behavior of the person at his side in the hope of his impossible change.

But when you get to the point where the suffering you have experienced becomes a source of somatic illness or illness, you usually start asking for help. Often, when one finds oneself in a relationship in which one suffers psychological violence and is unable to get out of it, one undertakes a path of individual psychotherapy: one turns to a psychologist or psychiatrist who tries to offer the employee another view of the relationship, another point of view that he had never evaluated.

Another strategy to address the problem of emotional dependence is the self-help group. The path of self-help is a powerful path, based on working in groups of people who share the same discomfort.

The group creates a space where each person can speak and tell their own experience without being judged and blocked. By sharing the discomfort you realize that you are not alone, and you can see and understand other ways of dealing with and experiencing the same problem.

Self-help groups are characterized by:

- small number of participants, usually maximum 10 people to facilitate interaction between subjects and the expression of their feelings;
- are organized on specific issues so that participants are equal: living or having experienced the same problem defines the group membership;
- share common goals: the energy and strength of the group are higher than the willingness to act individually;
- mutual help: everyone with their own experience, through confrontation and sharing, draws help for themselves and helps others;
- decisions, changes and rules are discussed and democratically accepted by all;
- communication is horizontal: everyone freely expresses their thoughts respecting others and without placing themselves at the centre of attention;
- each person decides autonomously if and when to take part in the group without being imposed by others: the person must be the protagonist of his own change to increase self-confidence and in his own abilities, therefore his own self-esteem.

The city of Cuneo offers an important resource for tackling the problem of emotional dependence. In fact, there is an association called "Il Cerchio" that has formed a self-help group for people who are in this condition, who have become aware of their problem and have found the courage to deal with it and solve it.

CHAPTER 3

AFFECTIVE REGULATION

Affective regulation is the set of processes through which the individual influences the emotions he experiences, when he experiences them, how he experiences them and how he expresses those emotions.

Each emotion is different from the others and has peculiar characteristics that make it unique. Usually, emotional experiences fluctuate below the threshold of awareness, even though they derive from concrete experiences. It often happens, for example, to feel a halo of sadness, or of anger, without knowing with certainty the causes. Emotions, in the first place, perform a function of homeostasis, and they do so outside of our awareness.

The transition from one emotional state to another occurs whenever necessary; in case of danger our brain forces us to feel fear and consequently our body activates all those processes essential to the protection of our health. It prepares our muscles to escape or attack, increases heartbeats and breathing, makes us much more reactive.

Affective regulation at this level therefore has an adaptive function. It allows us to adapt to the different environmental contexts in which we find ourselves, choosing for us the right emotions to feel depending on the circumstances.

There is a second level in which emotions are no longer closely linked to maintaining our internal balance and are involved in interpersonal relations. In this case, the regulation works according to ourselves and the other, where by other means we mean the people with whom we come into contact. Each individual with whom we interact causes in us the birth of certain emotions to which we respond in the way we consider most appropriate. Our interaction, what we say and do while we are with someone, is motivated by emotions. Without them, there would be no incentive to communicate, to make contact. At this level, therefore, affective regulation fulfils a motivational function towards our interaction with others.

It gives meaning, a meaning to what others do and to our own actions.

It prepares us to receive the stimuli addressed to us and at the same time provides us with the tools to give them meaning.

From this it is evident the importance of emotions and how each of our behavior is deeply influenced by our internal affective state. It is not possible to explain, therefore to understand, a behavior without referring to the emotional bases of such behavior.

Emotions are therefore essential integrative processes, which play a central role in conferring values and meanings and in linking the different activities and functions of the mind.

The regulation of emotions is the basis of the processes of self-organization, and the emotional communications that are established between parent and child profoundly influence the development of the child's ability to self-organize.

Patterns that are used in the transfer of energy and information between his mind and that of the parent can give rise to organized strategies, which manifest themselves with characteristic behavioral responses within the attachment relationship; his mind learns to adapt specifically to the type of emotional communication it receives from the adult, and with the passage of time these relationship-dependent patterns can become typical approaches that are used in more general contexts.

Different aspects of the regulation of emotions, such as the ability to adapt to stress, can be related to their attachment stories.

Conceptual bases of emotion regulation

The human brain has developed an intricate network of circuits that participate in modulating the states of emotional activation, or arousal. The nature of these regulatory processes varies significantly from individual to individual, with constitutional influences and adaptation to previous experiences. We can say with certainty that there are innate characteristics in each of us, introducing the term "emotional temperament". It refers to certain response patterns typical of each person. For example, there are people who tend to be calm and controlled and who rarely allow themselves to be overwhelmed by strong emotions, even in the face of important events. Others who react quickly and vivaciously to every slightest situational change.

These traits of the nervous system can still be modified in the course of existence.

They are built in childhood and their development is influenced by many variables. First of all, the parents' behaviour, through which the child can amplify and consolidate a certain type of emotional response, or on the contrary limit it. Let us take a constitutionally aggressive child as an example. A lascivious mother, unable to contain her son's abrupt temperament, can accentuate his aggressiveness. On the contrary, if it proves decisive and resolute, it can limit such behaviour.

Each of us reacts to emotions differently, however, there are some basic elements underlying emotional regulation that are common to all.

Intensity

Emotion processing is based on the activities of evaluation and arousal systems, which can respond to stimuli with different degrees of intensity.

In essence, our brain is able to vary the reaction to a given emotional stimulus by changing the number of activated neurons and the amount of neurotransmitters secreted.

If the initial orientation mechanisms lead to a minimal activation of the brain and body, the subsequent processing and arousal evaluation responses will also tend to be reduced.

In this regard, several studies have shown that individuals who were administered drugs to decrease the extent of responses of the body and the states of physiological activation generally reacted to stimuli by interpreting them as "unimportant", and therefore with primary emotions less intense than those of control subjects.

In each of us, the levels of intensity with which we generally respond to stimuli can be determined both by constitutional factors and by the influence of our previous experiences. People with a shy temperament, for example, tend to react with great intensity to unusual stimuli for them, implementing withdrawal and distancing behaviors. From some studies it seems that the intensity of emotional responses is related to a bilateral frontal activation, unlike their quality or valence, which is instead associated with asymmetric activations.

The right hemisphere is more involved in the states of estrangement, the left in the states of approach.

Research confirms that in children with clinically depressed mothers the ability to experience joy and excitement is significantly impaired, especially in cases where maternal depression persists after the first year of life of the child.

In children, therefore, experiences can profoundly influence both the intensity and the value of emotional activations. In particular, in those with depressed parents, there may be no experiences of sharing positive emotional states, experiences that in normal conditions allow the parent-child couple to amplify pleasant emotions and to experience waves of intense mutual affection.

The lack of this shared amplification of positive states can negatively affect the development of the ability to tolerate and appreciate intense emotional states: interactive experiences allow the child not only to experience high levels of emotional "tension" or arousal, but also to "train" his brain circuits to handle such states.

The intensity of emotional responses is often masked because it coincides with the moment of greatest need to be understood by others, generating a sense of vulnerability that can make us reluctant to manifest our feelings openly.

This behaviour is amplified by unsatisfactory interpersonal communication experiences and can give rise to a sense of shame for missing an opportunity for emotional attunement.

Sensitivity

The threshold of sensitivity is different in each individual. This is the minimum level below which sensations and stimuli do not induce an activation of our evaluation systems.

Those who have a very low emotional threshold are constantly faced with emotionally engaging situations considered important. Like intensity, sensitivity is also influenced by both constitutional and experiential factors, and at the same time can be influenced by what is the state of the mind at that time.

For example, when we say that we have "nerves on top of our skin" we mean that at that precise moment we are very sensitive to any slight environmental variation, thus providing exaggerated answers.

How can our brain change the sensitivity threshold? First of all, it should be borne in mind that emotions are inextricably linked to the processes of evaluating stimuli. The brain can directly increase or decrease its sensitivity to the environment by raising or lowering the levels of stimulation needed to activate its evaluation systems. If we have just seen a violent and scary film, we can be very sensitive to dark alleys and loud noises, for example. If we hear the sound of a burst coming out of the cinema, we can easily scare ourselves and evaluate the situation as dangerous. If we have the same experience coming back from a party with friends it is likely that our reaction is not the same. Recent experiences can therefore directly influence our degree of emotional sensitivity (Schacter, Buckner, 1998).

In the same way, the repetition of emotionally intense experiences can generate chronic alterations in the degree of sensitivity.

Terrorising episodes experienced during childhood can permanently change an individual's sensitivity to stimuli related to such traumatic events.

If a child is scratched and bitten by a cat, it is possible that even after years the sight of a cat evokes in him an intense emotional response of fear.

Early alterations of the brain circuits involved in the processes of evaluation and attribution of meanings can therefore have profound effects on the mechanisms that directly influence the nature of emotional experiences and the regulation of emotions.

The state of hypersensitivity that is generated in this way is often irreversible, however, it is possible to intervene on the phase of evaluation of the stimulus that originates from the state of excessive general arousal, making the patient's reaction more "elastic".

Specificity

Regulatory processes can also determine which regions of the brain are activated in states of emotional arousal.

By defining the specificity of evaluation processes

- the way in which evaluation centres establish the meaning of representations
- the brain is able to regulate energy flows in changes in system states.

For example, if we are awakened by a sudden noise during rest, it is likely that our body will enter a state of initial orientation.

If we were waiting for a friend to arrive, the noise might induce a pleasant excitement in us. If we weren't waiting for anyone, it could be a warning sign. The representations that are activated at any given moment, including those that refer to the context of the situation in which we find ourselves, help to define the specific direction of the evaluation of a stimulus, and therefore the type of emotional response that is evoked.

The specificity of evaluation processes directly influences the differentiation of primary emotional states into fundamental emotions, and individual differences in evaluation mechanisms and parameters can influence the overall "nature" of mood and personality.

This specificity determines not only the meaning of the emotional processes themselves, through mechanisms of "evaluation of evaluation".

The specificity of these processes may be influenced by several factors related to the interpretation of the stimulus; for example, whether or not it is assessed as relevant to the achievement of present and future objectives, or by the meaning attributed to it with respect to general issues concerning the Self or the Self in relation to others.

As the child grows, the differentiation of primary emotions into fundamental emotions becomes increasingly sophisticated, and early states of generic "well-being" or "malaise" are gradually replaced by fundamental emotions such as fear, anger, disgust, surprise, interest, shame or joy. From this perspective, in the differentiation of its emotional processes, the mind of the child integrates inner processes and interactive responses of the parents; in this way, the most differentiated emotions become attractors of the system, with constraints determined by internal and external factors.

The specificity of an emotional experience is determined by the complex mechanisms of evaluation that are selectively activated in response to a particular stimulus.

In each of us the development of these evaluation processes is influenced both by constitutional characteristics and by factors linked to the history of our social interactions, and this is why when faced with the same stimulus two people can sometimes react in a completely different way; the specificity of our emotional responses creates unique personal meanings.

Emotions have been defined and classified in various ways. Some scholars distinguish, for example, the main categories represented by fear, surprise/dismay, sadness, anger, pleasure/joy, interest/excitement, disgust, anxiety, distrust, contempt, love; other types of emotion are embarrassment, shame, guilt, pride. Throughout our lives we have all experienced each of these emotions and we have certainly noticed how each time the same emotion presents itself with different characteristics; these characteristics are determined by the uniqueness of the combinations between internal processes and external contexts in which that particular state of the system develops.

The complex evaluation processes must have been organized by at least two fundamental factors.

According to the essential principles of evolutionary theory, the characteristics of evaluation systems that increased the probability of survival and transmission of the genetic make-up tended to be maintained. This could explain, for example, why some people are afraid of snakes even though they have never seen one in their lives.

A second crucial component from an evolutionary point of view is that evaluation mechanisms must be able to learn from past experiences.

By assessing a situation as dangerous, we can avoid it and save ourselves unnecessary risks. Evaluation systems can learn from experience; emotional processes promote learning.

Tolerance windows

The tolerance window is the margin within which emotional states of different intensities can be processed without compromising the functioning of the system as a whole. Each of us has different windows of tolerance.

Some people are able to handle high levels of emotional intensity without any difficulty and retain the ability to think, act and feel in a balanced and effective way. However, there are emotions such as anger or sadness that even at moderate levels can negatively interfere with the activities of the mind. The intensity of a specific emotional state can involve mechanisms of evaluation and arousal that are not accessible by consciousness and that can influence the processes of information processing. Emotional activation states that exceed the window of tolerance can generate disorganized thoughts and behaviors.

In some individuals the window can be very narrow, and emotional processes can only become conscious when their degree of intensity is very close to the levels beyond which these disorganizing effects are produced.

In others, the mind system can tolerate even very intense emotional states, which are easily accessible to the consciousness, regardless of their pleasant nature (in the case of joy or love) or unpleasant (anger, sadness).

It should also be considered that the width of the window varies over time depending on the state of the mind, the specific emotional value and the social context in which the emotion is generated. For example, we are able to handle situations that generate stress more effectively when we are in the presence of people to whom we are attached, who understand and love us.

This can be explained in terms of activity of the autonomic nervous system. Excessive activity in the sympathetic system results in an increase in heart and respiratory rates and a feeling of generalised tension.

On the contrary, excessive activation of the parasympathetic system produces processes that tend to save energy, decreasing heartbeats, breathing and mental activity.

Sometimes the two systems are activated at the same time inducing feeling of "loss of control", as if we were driving the car and push accelerator and brake together.

Under these conditions, superior brain function is impaired.

Rational thinking becomes impossible and automatic and reflected reactions prevail; the integrative functions of emotions, in which self-regulating processes allow elastic and adaptive interactions with the environment, are temporarily suspended.

The limits of a person's tolerance window are determined both by constitutional characteristics (temperament) and previous experiences, and are heavily influenced by contingent physiological conditions; for example, hunger and thirst make us particularly irritable and emotionally vulnerable.

Constitutionally shy people may find themselves deeply uncomfortable in the face of intense emotions of any kind, and tend to look for familiar environments, which do not evoke these disturbing and disorganizing feelings; in the context of social contexts that provide for the closeness of attachment figures with whom they have secure relationships are able to deal with situations for them new, but in the absence of such conditions may take away behavior and become socially isolated.

At the other end of the spectrum are people who, in situations that are new to them, experience a sense of pleasure and excitement without affecting their internal balance. Children who have this second type of attitude, more open and exploratory towards the outside world, generally make life easier for their parents; on the contrary, those with more difficult, irritable and capricious temperaments often have reactions that go beyond the margins of their window of tolerance, becoming a serious problem for parents. However, in the majority of cases, these growing children develop more and more sophisticated capacities to regulate emotions, and their "emotional outbursts" become less frequent.

The windows of tolerance are also influenced by the history of past experiences. For example, in individuals who have often had experiences of fear in childhood, this emotion can be associated with a profoundly disorganizing sense of terror and dismay; the repeated feeling of being left alone to deal with these emotions, without anyone who can comfort and reassure them, can lead to a failure to develop the ability to calm and control these states, and to a reduction in the limits of tolerance.

The tolerance window of an individual also depends on what his state of mind is at a given time.

If we feel emotionally "exhausted", physically exhausted or surprised by an unexpected interaction, it is likely that our margins of tolerance have diminished. In these conditions we can become tense and agitated, and be visibly disturbed by stimuli to which we normally react with more contained emotions.

Return processes within tolerance margins

When the intensity of a state of arousal exceeds the boundaries of the window of tolerance, the mind can be submerged by a wave of emotions that involves a whole series of processes, from rational thinking to social behavior, and that can also overwhelm the consciousness.

In situations of this kind, the individual often has the feeling of having lost control of thoughts and actions, and his mind can be invaded by visual representations that symbolize the emotional state.

For example, when they are angry, some may literally "see red", or have images of themselves attacking the object of their anger, and perform violent and destructive acts that in normal conditions are not part of their behavioral repertoire.

Emotions, meanings and social interactions are mediated by the brain circuits themselves; the way in which this information is processed depends on the biological reality of the structures of the brain, which directly shape the functions of the mind.

For example, at the level of the orbital-frontal cortex, one of the central regions in the processing of emotions, converge inputs that come from anatomically distinct areas, and information involving social cognitive processes, autonomous consciousness, sensations, perceptions, representations of various kinds such as words, concepts, somatic markers that refer to the physiological states of the organism and the activities of the autonomous nervous system.

The ability to respond adaptively to the personal meaning of an event, and not simply with an automatic and reflected reaction, is based on the ability to flexibly integrate these prefrontal processes.

It is believed that in states of excessive arousal the "superior" processes mediated by neocortical circuits are instead suspended, and that the direction of energy flows within the brain, and in particular at the level of the orbital-frontal regions, are determined mainly by inputs generated by "inferior" structures of information processing (brainstem centers, sensory circuits, limbic areas).

In this way, the overcoming of the tolerance window is accompanied, at the neurological level, by an inhibition of the superior perceptive and rational mechanisms, while the more "elementary" somatic and sensory activities assume a dominant role. We no longer think: we "feel" intensely and act impulsively; in other words, we enter a state in which potentially prevail reflected responses to primary somatic and sensory stimuli.

But how does the mind "recover" from states in which superior cortical functions and the ability to reflect on one's own thoughts and behaviors are suspended? These processes of recovery vary from individual to individual, and once again depend, in addition to the constitutional characteristics and personal history, on the context and nature of the specific state.

For example, if we feel betrayed by a friend we trusted blindly, being able to re-emerge from a state of deep anger and sadness can be particularly difficult, while disappointments generated by people we are less attached to, or recognized as tending to be unreliable, can induce reactions of anger that are quickly disposed of.

To get out of these states the mind must reduce the disorganizing effects produced by a particular episode of emotional arousal. This can be done through basic physiological processes, in which the evaluation mechanisms report the activation levels within tolerable margins by decreasing the intensity of the arousal state and limiting the number of neuronal circuits and groups involved.

More complex cortical functions can also be progressively reactivated, allowing metacognitive processes of self-reflection and impulse control; in general, the ability to reflect on one's own mental states and those of others plays an important role in this particular aspect of emotion regulation.

An even partial recovery of these cortical activities may allow the individual to alter the characteristics of the emotional state and to endure previously uncontrollable levels of arousal.

For example, overwhelmed by anger at the friend who has deceived us, we can discover that recalling old

memories of our past relationship with him we can transform the nature and intensity of this emotional experience, replacing anger with a sense of loss and great sadness that we can more easily tolerate. However, for some people controlling excessively intense emotional states can be extremely difficult, regardless of their nature; for these people life can become a continuous series of efforts to avoid situations that could generate too strong emotions, in an attempt to defend and maintain the balance of their system. Such individuals may become slaves to their own emotional instability.

Emotions play a central role in the processes of self-regulation of the mind. It is inevitable that emotional arousal processes sometimes exceed our threshold of tolerance, whatever it may be; in the absence of effective recovery processes, however, these moments can turn into prolonged states of disorganization, which can be dangerous for us and for others.

The ability to fall within the limits of the tolerance window, in essence, allows the self-organizing processes of the system to return to a flow of states that move in a balanced manner towards greater

complexity, avoiding, at the two extremes, excessively rigid activations or excessively random and chaotic. The mind system thus becomes more adaptive, tuning in to internal and external variables in a more flexible way, and increasing its levels of complexity and stability.

CHAPTER 4

Access to consciousness

At all times the activities of our evaluation systems influence all the functions of the mind, through mechanisms that do not necessarily require the participation of the consciousness. Emotions are a set of fundamental processes directly related to the attribution of meanings, social communication, attentional mechanisms and the elaboration of perceptions.

Emotions direct the activation flows (energy) and establish the meaning of the representations (information) and therefore have a central role in determining the activities of the system of the mind as a whole.

A large amount of data supports the idea that only a small part of our mental activities take place on a conscious level.

Perception, memory, emotions, social interactions are all processes that occur mostly outside of consciousness.

These unconscious processes form the basis of the functions of the mind, deeply influencing our feelings, thoughts and behaviors, and may suddenly emerge in our conscious mind (for example when we start to cry even before we become aware of feeling a sense of sadness).

In general, we can say that the Self is not formed by a conscious part and an unconscious part, separated by a clear line of demarcation; rather, the Self is created by unconscious processes, and by the selective association of these processes in an entity that we call "consciousness".

In other words, we are much, much more than our conscious processes.

What is the use of conscience? The possible answers are different, including the one according to which the processes that are connected within the consciousness can be manipulated and altered intentionally, in order to produce more adaptive responses.

Consciousness allows us to modify automatic and reflected reactions and to introduce elements of "choice" into our behaviour. When something upsets us and we know the cause, we can actively intervene to solve the problem.

Consciousness is linked to attentional mechanisms and working memory. This memory is a kind of temporary storage that allows us to keep in mind and reflect simultaneously on a series of different information and data. These reflections allow us to manipulate the various representations, to elaborate them further and to establish new associations between them. Through this system, working memory allows processes of self-reflection and cognitive "choices"; in other words, it makes possible personal intentions and deliberate and strategic behaviors, which are not the result of automatic reflexes.

Emotional processes - the initial orientation phase, the mechanisms of arousal and evaluation, the differentiation of primary states - generally take place outside of consciousness; awareness of these processes manifests itself with the qualitative sensations associated with emotions, and with the whole range of what we can call our "feelings". Feelings" therefore involve energy, behavioural impulses, meanings or fundamental emotions.

They reach the level of consciousness because they allow us to attribute meanings to what we are experiencing and consequently allow us to respond more flexibly to environmental stimuli.

Moreover, the awareness of our emotions is fundamental for our very survival as social beings: it allows us to recognize intentions and motivations, ours and those of others, and to manage the complex interactions with the interpersonal world in a more effective and appropriate way to meet our needs and achieve our goals.

Consciousness can influence the outcome of emotional processes: it allows processes of self-reflection, which in turn make it possible to mobilize thoughts and behaviors that facilitate the achievement of particular goals, through the acquisition of new levels of integration. For example, if we are aware that we are sad because a friend of ours has moved to another city, we may decide to call him, or write him a letter; on the contrary, if our sadness remains unconscious it is possible that we will never try to re-establish contact with this person. Consciousness therefore plays the important role of modulating energy flows within the brain, involving brain structures responsible for processing these flows, thus achieving a higher level of integration.

This leads to an adaptive response that goes far beyond the simple automatic or reflected reaction.

Evaluation processes lead to the activation of distinct neural groups in the creation of a certain state of mind; the participation of consciousness in this set of activations allows the recruitment of new associations within the working memory, the blackboard of the mind. By involving linguistic systems and autonomous functions, consciousness allows us to reflect on the past and the future, and thus to go beyond the limits of what are our experiences of the moment. Being aware of our emotions also allows us to develop more appropriate responses to the achievement of specific goals, which would not be possible without the participation of consciousness.

External Expressions

From the very first days of life, emotions constitute both the tools and the contents of the communications that are established between parent and child.

To put it in very simple terms, the internal state of the child is perceived by the parents, who tune in to that state; the child in turn perceives the response of the parents, and a mutual emotional agreement is created.

Later parents can also use words to define feelings and states of the child's mind; they can say, for example, that he feels happy, scared or sad, providing the child with an interactive verbal experience that allows him to identify and share his emotional state.

These early forms of communication allow the child to develop the "idea" that his emotional life can be shared with others, in relationships that can be a source of security and comfort.

Within the second year of their life, children generally learn to hide their emotions in certain social contexts. For example, if he strongly wants something, but has learned that the fact that he shows an interest in the object in question inevitably arouses reactions of anger from parents, the child may find it wiser to take an impassive attitude, which does not reveal the true nature of his emotional state.

In adults, these "concealment" abilities are generally highly developed, and allow us to act in a more socially appropriate way, disguising emotions that may induce criticism or harsh reactions from other people. Culture and the family environment play a central role in determining how the child learns these often unwritten conventions and norms that govern emotional expression, often referred to by some as "exhibition rules".

Studies conducted in different populations and cultures show that children and adults can express their emotions in very different ways if they are alone or in the presence of strangers. But if cultural norms in certain situations tell us not to express our emotions, can this negatively affect the way we become aware of our emotional responses? In fact, it would seem so; as we have seen before, our brain creates representations that refer to the body's reaction and uses them as information that allows it to verify "how we feel".

The Self is capable of at least two contextual states: an "internal" private self and an "external", public and adaptive self. Some authors also speak of a "true" or "false" Self; however, these terms imply the idea that adaptation behaviors are to be considered in some way false, while in general it may be more useful simply to accept the fact that, in each of us, different contexts may evoke different states.

In certain social situations the ability to hide one's emotions can be adaptively important: there is nothing "false" about a survival mechanism.

On the other hand, since our brains often rely on external expressions to understand what we feel, these dissimulation processes can clearly make access to what are our "true" emotional responses more difficult.

Through internal and external mechanisms, the regulation of emotional expressions can help the mind to modulate its activation states, and to keep them within the limits of the tolerance window. At a social level, by disguising our emotions we can, for example, avoid experiences of interpersonal resonance that would lead to an alteration of our state of mind, or the risk of not being understood and the consequent sense of shame and frustration. Internally, the control of emotional manifestations allows us to reduce the effects of positive feedback mechanisms through which facial expressions and body responses, once perceived by the mind, determine a further intensification of the emotional state that initially generated them.

Problems arise when these modulation processes are excessively rigid, and the inhibition of emotional expressions becomes a typical state, a trait of the individual.

If in the course of its development the child does not find social contexts in which the private Self can interact freely and fully with other people, the public and adaptive Self can become dominant; its emotions are systematically disguised and hidden not only from others, but also from itself. By repeatedly blocking his emotional expressions, the individual runs the risk of chronically inhibiting the access of emotions to consciousness; these people may have the feeling that they do not really know "who they are", and that their lives are meaningless. The mechanisms that cause a blockage of emotional expressions are not clear, but probably involve a temporary inhibition of the circuits that control these expressions, located mainly in the right hemisphere, and particularly at the level of the amygdala and the orbital-frontal cortex. For example, people with injuries to the right hemisphere may have a reduced ability both to express their emotional states and to perceive their own emotions and those of others.

Brain imaging studies conducted on depressed subjects also found in these patients, who showed decreased facial expression, the existence of a functional block in the activation of the centers of the right hemisphere responsible for the perception of faces. These observations indicate that the manifestation and perception of emotions through facial expressions could therefore be neurobiologically related processes.

The ability to express one's emotions varies greatly from individual to individual.

The manifestation of primary emotional states is mainly based on non-verbal signals, such as facial expressions, tones of voice, gestures and movements of the limbs, and on the ways (timing, fluidity) in which these messages agree with those transmitted by another person. If the individual is aware of the signals he sends and receives, he can more easily modify his state of mind in relation to that of the person in front of him; he can reflect on his sensations, and this can be essential to help him understand the emotions of the other.

The fact of feeling "understood" in the deepest sense of the term, of having the feeling that others feel the same emotions as us and are able to respond directly and immediately to our communications, is a fundamental ingredient of our attachment relationships, in childhood as well as in adulthood.

These forms of interpersonal interaction allow the establishment of states of affective attunement that favour the amplification of positive emotions and the reduction of negative emotions; within relationships of safe attachment, they allow the child to develop the self-regulating abilities necessary to control and diminish the impact of "unpleasant" states of mind.

Affective regulation and the mind

The modulation of the processes of evaluation and arousal plays a fundamental role in the organization of the mind. The ability to regulate emotions emerges early, in relationships of secure attachment, where collaborative forms of communication and "reflective" dialogues allow the child to develop internal coherence and mentalizing functions.

Self-organization is acquired within interpersonal experiences of affective attunement, which allow the amplification of positive emotional states and facilitate the control of negative emotions; through these dyadic resonance states the child learns to communicate and share his emotions, and to widen his margins of tolerance.

The seven essential aspects of emotion regulation - intensity, sensitivity, specificity, windows of tolerance, processes of returning within the margins of tolerance, access to consciousness and external expressions - are linked both to constitutional components (temperament) and to the history of our attachment relationships. In our first years of life "epigenetic" factors, and in particular social experiences that influence the gene expression and the experience-dependent maturation of our brain structures, have direct effects on the way in which the neural circuits involved in the modulation of emotions develop; in adulthood, the same elements of attachment within interpersonal relationships can contribute to the development of new capacities of self-organization. Many forms of mental illness can be considered as the result of states of emotional dysregulation.

Such states can manifest with sudden explosions of emotions, such as anger, sadness, or terror, that exceed the limits of the window of tolerance and overwhelm the capacities of rational thinking, flexibility of response, and self-reflection; the individual has the feeling of having "lost control", and his internal and interpersonal activities are compromised. To be able to help these people it is necessary to try to favour the development of more effective processes of self-organization, and in this sense the acquisition of greater metacognitive abilities and a reflective mentalizing function can be very important. Constitutional characteristics, traumatic experiences or non-optimal attachment relationships can produce a maladaptive regulation of emotions, which limits the emotional resistance and behavioural flexibility of the individual; if the ability of the limbic system to modulate intense states of arousal is reduced, it may be particularly useful to learn to use neocortical functions that allow to analyze, and therefore to intervene, on the initial dysregulatory responses. In other words, when a person goes beyond his or her margins of tolerance, he or she loses the ability to think rationally; modifying the initial automatic reactions can be very difficult, especially when it comes to rooted responses, which were inscribed early in his or her limbic circuits. However, strategies involving neocortical activities can help the individual to bring the intensity of these emotional responses back to more tolerable levels (e.g. through internal reflective dialogues, or by evoking the "soothing" image of an attachment figure), and to make them less frequent and easier to control.

Emotions and integrative processes

One of the main characteristics of the mind is its ability to connect and coordinate, at any given time and over time, processes of various kinds in a coherent set of activities; to define the functions on which this ability is based, in disciplines that study different aspects of mental life - from social psychology to neuroscience - the term "integration" is used. Within the brain, the coordination of activities involving distinct neural circuits allows the emergence of complex functions.

Limbic and associative regions play a central role in these neural integration processes, in particular the frontal areas such as the orbital-frontal cortex, which are widely connected to various brain areas. The mechanisms of the frontal lobe are not yet completely clear, but it is known that they link the activities of the frontal cortex to the different systems of regulation of the brain, from those that control arousal levels through projections of the brain stem to the recessed cortico-limbic interactions involved in memory control.

When sufficiently clarified, these mechanisms will prove to be central not only in the modulation of the physiological processes of nerve tissue, but also in the representation and maintenance of the Self.

The mechanisms of neural integration are therefore fundamental to the processes of self-organization, and to the ability of the brain to create a sense of self. This form of integration may involve associative neurons that connect anatomically and functionally distinct systems; when processes mediated by regions on both sides of the brain are connected, the terms "bilateral integration" or "interhemispheric" may be used.

The fact that "the highest level of integration of sensory, motor and evaluative processes can be achieved in the primitive prembic cortex" has led Tucker and collaborators to suggest the possibility that these three forms of integration, in each of which activities mediated by this brain region are involved, are actually interdependent.

For example, vertical integration mechanisms are the basis of the right hemisphere's ability to have predominant control over certain "lower" functions, such as the representation and regulation of body activities mediated by the autonomic nervous system, while lateral integration processes are involved, during REM sleep phases, in the recording and recall mechanisms in which the right and left orbital-frontal cortices are involved in vertical and lateral integration activities; Future studies will be needed to clarify whether and how this brain region also participates in dorsal-ventral integration mechanisms, in one or both sides of the brain.

This means that the brain is able to create, in the present, patterns of neuronal activity in which influences generated by past experiences are incorporated.

The organization of memory processes allows the brain to function as a machine that tries to "represent the future" on the basis of past events; these mechanisms of "anticipation" directly influence the way in which links can be established between different processes at a given time and over time.

It creates complex representations through processes of spatial-temporal integration between perceptions (input) and actions (output), in an attempt to interact with an environment that changes in time and space.

These representational processes allow us to evaluate different situations more quickly, to understand what the immediate future most likely holds for us, and to act in a more adaptive way, increasing our chances of survival; in this sense, the mechanisms of integration can be considered as fundamental processes in the evolution of the human mind. Experiences result in neuronal activations that can induce gene transcription processes and changes in synaptic connections. The information is transmitted through the involvement of the distinct neural circuits in clusters of activations that are functionally connected, and this leads to the creation of further representations and new states of mind.

When new information processing elements are incorporated into a new state of the system, the binding of these different elements into a unified functional whole is the essence of the integration processes.

Precisely on the basis of these fundamental neuronal mechanisms it happens that particularly rooted states of the mind may or may not be integrated in the general flow of the complex states of the system. For example, insecure forms of attachment may be associated with multiple and inconsistent internal operating patterns, and with poorly flexible states of mind - such as states of fear or shame - that are not integrated over time and that give rise to specific, potentially dysfunctional states of the Self. We can hypothesize that in these cases the creation of new neuronal connections leads to an alteration of the constraints of the dynamic system of the brain, with changes that can favour the integration of functionally independent and isolated states, which interfere with its capacity to adapt.

Emotions play a central role in these integration processes. As we have already seen, Emotions are intrinsically integrative processes, which link together internal processes and different individuals, and which are involved in an important way in the mechanisms of self-regulation and in the communications that are established within interpersonal relationships.

It is not possible to discuss the integrative functions of the brain without taking into account the more complex activities generated by neural systems, and it would be unreasonable not to identify the emotions among the critical integrative components that operate at this level. Nevertheless, throughout the twentieth century, the brain and the integrated mind have often been discussed, almost completely ignoring the very existence of emotions, and not only neglecting their fundamental functions or the importance of understanding their neurobiological bases. (Damasio)

Emotionally significant events can allow our minds to continue to learn throughout the course of our existence. In these learning mechanisms, experiences play an essential role, stimulating the formation of new synaptic connections and fostering development processes that can continue throughout the life of the individual, and also involve the neural circuits involved in integrative functions.

Neurons that mediate the coordination of information generated by distinct brain regions may continue to develop in ways determined by genetic programs and specific forms of experience. Experiences and innate processes can thus allow our brain to continue to develop its capacity for integration, through mechanisms of differentiation of neural circuits involving a whole series of different processes: axon growth, formation of new synaptic connections and increase in the speed of conduction of nerve fibers linked to an increase in their myelination. The movement towards greater integration is in accordance with the theory of complexity: the presence of highly differentiated and functionally linked subsystems allows the system to reach higher levels of complexity. In this sense, a progressive increase in the degree of differentiation and integration of the various brain functions during the entire course of our existence can be considered as the natural result of development processes. We can imagine that in some of us such processes over the years lead, for example, to greater "wisdom", to the integrative ability to recognize general patterns in different experiences and situations, rather than focusing on the details that characterize individual events. On the contrary, different forms of mental disorder can emerge from internal or external processes and constraints - linked to constitutional factors, experiences or interpersonal relationships - that interfere with this natural movement towards greater integration, fixing the flow of the system in maladaptive directions that lead to excessively rigid or chaotic states.

We can therefore think that a "healthy" and balanced development is fed by internal processes and interpersonal relationships that promote a continuous differentiation of the various components of the mind system, and at the same time their integration.

Emotions and flows of energy and information within the system are the basis of these integration processes, which allow a continuous development in the single mind and minds of multiple individuals interacting with each other.

In our relationships with others, individual differentiation and interpersonal integration allow our minds to continue to "grow" in a complex biological interdependence of our internal and social worlds.

CHAPTER 5

AFFECTIVE CHILD ATTACHMENT AND REGULATION

In children, the first behavioural manifestations that we can grasp are those of attachment. The child is genetically predisposed to develop a bond of attachment with those who take care of him in search of protection, for an innate need, perhaps a drive, functional to his survival. Attachment is one of the behavioural control systems that motivates the child to approach the caregiver to maintain a sense of security. Attachment behaviours are already visible, at birth, in the auditory, olfactory, tactile and cenoesthetic recognition of the mother by the newborn child; at the second to third month of life they then become a capacity for proposal and response when the child is able to recognize familiar people and interact with them in a differentiated way. From the eighth month onwards, there are clear indications of a well-developed and long-lasting bond of attachment: the child engages in behaviours of approaching and seeking contact with family members, while being afraid of strangers.

From the end of the first year of life, with the clear signs given through social referencing and understanding of the theory of the other's mind, he enters a phase of decisively directed attachment, in which he behaves intentionally, plans his actions according to the objectives, takes into account feelings, motivations and objectives of the other through the understanding of the state of mind and becomes, therefore, able to flexibly use the means of social reporting to achieve his goals. Among the attachment behaviors at the end of the first year of life, individual differences emerge. These differences reflect the temperamental diversity, i.e. the different activation and predisposition to express emotions, but also the model of emotional-cognitive regulation that developed between the caregiver and the child during the first year of life. The attachment behaviors manifested by the child are, that is, the result of the quality of the early attachment interactions and determine the way in which the subject processes the information.

Towards the end of the first year of life, with the appearance of symbolisation, an internal model of one's attachment relationships is formed.

This mental representation, defined as the internal operative model, includes: the operative model of the Self, that is the image that the subject has of himself, the concept of how much it is acceptable or not in the eyes of others; the operative model of the world, that consists in the representation of the subject about the external reality; the assumptions about how interpersonal relations work. On the basis of this mnestic structure the child creates expectations about the figures of attachment, their responsiveness and accessibility, learns to predict and understand how to get the closeness and support of others and how to move in the social world. These models are therefore a guide for the actions of the child: they enable him to anticipate the behavior of the other and to plan an appropriate line of response. Since the internal operating model is the internalization of early interactive experiences, a child who knows how to express his needs adequately, grown up with a sensitive and available caregiver, develops self-esteem, trust in others, positive expectations of interpersonal relationships; conversely, a child who has experienced frightened, uncertain, inconstant or otherwise inadequate caregivers, develops a limited or discontinuous self-esteem, sometimes hypertrophic, a mistrust of other people and negative expectations of relationships.

These two modes summarize the two basic types of attachment: secure and insecure attachment. It should be added, however, that, contrary to what has been stated by most studies on attachment, subjects who have a secure attachment, but who have created themselves in an "easy" situation, will have more difficulty in finding vital solutions in cases of emergency, which will instead, in many cases, be more easily addressed by insecure people who are already accustomed to defending themselves.

Parent-child relationship and emotional development

The child must develop the ability to regulate his physical and mental states; through processes of emotional communication and "alignment" of states of mind, responds to the neural activation patterns of parents through mechanisms of "internalization", which allow the activities of the brain more mature than the adult to directly shape the development of its neuronal systems.

Emotional tuning processes create connections between the minds of the parent and child that are essential in allowing the child's brain to acquire the ability to modulate and organize its functions in an increasingly autonomous way.

By acting as an intermediary between the brain and the body, the autonomic nervous system directly participates in the control of arousal conditions. Through the sympathetic system it can induce states of excitement and hypervigilance, associated with a high energy expenditure, with responses that may include, for example, an increase in heart rate, respiratory rhythms and sweating.

The parasympathetic system, on the other hand, generally has an inhibitory action, which favours energy saving; its activation leads to a slowing down of the heart rate and of the respiratory rate, and to a reduced vigilance and reactivity towards environmental stimuli.

During the first year of life, the development of the sympathetic system is dominant, while the parasympathetic system becomes progressively more active from the second year; when the child begins to walk, it becomes essential to have the possibility of modulating the primary emotional states mediated by the sympathetic system (interest, excitement, joy) in order to control and prevent potentially dangerous behaviour. During the first months of the child's life, the sharing and amplification of these positive states, which can be considered as a form of resonance of the activities of the sympathetic systems of parent and child, constitutes an essential and dominant part of their emotional communications. Later, however, it is necessary for parents to intervene with prohibitions and prohibitions aimed at inhibiting such "activating" emotional states, which in certain situations can jeopardize the safety of the child; for example, if a child is very young and tries to climb a ladder, it is important that he has learned the meaning of the word "No!": "Do not do it; stop immediately".

But how is it possible that the states of mind of parent and child come into tune if the child is learning that the parent may not share his or her excitement about what he or she is doing?

In fact, the search for a balance between the need to share her mental states and the prohibitions of her parents is one of the main aspects of the development of the child's self-regulating abilities.

The shame is the emotion that the child feels when a state of arousal does not correspond to a similar response from the parent; to some extent it is an essential emotion, inevitable and necessary, which helps him to learn to regulate his states of mind and his behavioral impulses. It is thought that this form of shame is generated by the activation of the parasympathetic system (in response to an external "No!") in the framework of an arousal state supported by the sympathetic system (an internal "Strength, let's go!"); it is as if after having pressed the accelerator pedal (the sympathetic system) we suddenly pressed the brake pedal (the parasympathetic system) too. A feeling of shame is therefore not simply the product of parasympathetic activities, but requires a dynamic situation in which a high sympathetic tone is followed by an activation of the parasympathetic system.

According to Schore shame is linked to a lack of "emotional connection": the child actively tries to reach a state of emotional attunement, but these attempts are frustrated by the parent. In this specific sense it is not in itself a negative emotion; on the contrary, it contributes significantly to the development of self-control abilities that allow the child to modulate emotions and behaviour according to the social context. However, interactions that induce a sense of shame and are followed by a repair of parent-child communications, or that are accompanied by prolonged manifestations of anger on the part of the adult, lead to the establishment of states of humiliation, emotion that has characters other than shame and that would instead have adverse effects on the maturation of the brain of the child.

The orbital-frontal cortex, situated in a key position at the limits of the limbic emotional system and in close proximity to the associative cortical areas responsible for the "superior" functions of thought and consciousness, plays a fundamental role in affective regulation. Involved in an important way in evaluation processes, this brain region, which is particularly sensitive to forms of communication mediated by looks and facial expressions, directly influences the way in which arousal states are processed in various types of emotional experiences.

Before better analyzing the role of the orbital-frontal cortex, it is good to clarify the concept of "affective tuning".

This expression refers to the communications that occur between parent and child, and in particular to the state of correspondence between the "psychobiological states" of the adult-child dyad that is created during these interactions. Other related terms are "alignment" and "resonance". By alignment we mean a component of the processes of affective tuning, in which the state of one individual is modified to agree with that of the other; it can therefore be a unilateral process, in which only one member of the couple alters his state in function of that of the other, or biunivocal, with the active participation of both individuals involved. For example, a parent may try to put an excited child to sleep; his or her attempts will almost certainly have a greater chance of success if he or she manages to get closer at first to his or her child's emotional state, and then gradually calm him or her down, instead of simply expecting the child to calm down on his or her own: the parent's initial one-way alignment allows the child to more easily reach a state of calm. The processes of affective tuning also lead to the establishment of what is defined as "resonance", the state in which the minds of two individuals influence each other. An emotional resonance, for example, does not only involve an agreement of emotional states, but includes how this affects other aspects and activities of the mind.

The resonance continues even after the alignment; in this way the affective tuning is based on an alternation of moments of alignment and non-alignment of the states of the mind, and allows an emotional resonance that persists even when the two individuals are no longer in direct communication.

In other words, moments of rupture in emotional communication between parent and child induce an activation of the parasympathetic system, while a subsequent realignment leads to the reactivation of the sympathetic system, associated with more appropriate and acceptable levels of arousal; energy flows within the child's mind are modulated and channeled in new directions.

The little one learns that what he is doing does not please his parents, but if he changes it they will still connect with him, so in the end everything will be fine. This creates a balance between brakes and accelerator, and this balance constitutes the essence of the processes of affective regulation.

The margins of tolerance towards the levels of activation of the autonomic nervous system can vary significantly from individual to individual; the overcoming of these limits, with the establishment of excessive states of arousal (the sympathetic system) or inhibition (the parasympathetic system), can be associated with a reduction in the ability to respond flexibly and adaptively to the environment, and have negative effects on the functions and development of the brain.

Parental responses

The way in which the parent responds to the child's challenging behaviour and attitudes defines the general tone of interactions within the couple, and directly influences the development of the child's ability to regulate his or her emotions and states of mind. Let's consider, for example, a fourteen-month-old child who wants to climb a table with a lamp on it. In such a situation, the mother can react in many different ways. He can shout "No!", and then take the child to the garden, where the child can more freely vent his desire to move and explore, or he may not realize that the child is trying to get on the table, hear the sound of the lamp falling on the floor, pick it up, quietly tell the child not to do it again or just ignore it for the rest of the day.

Alternatively, she can scream "No!" and then yell at him harshly, then feel guilty and embrace him; finally, decide to push him away again to make him understand that she is not happy with him.

In a fourth possible answer the mother could instead go terribly angry and throw the lamp violently on the floor, near the feet of the child, to teach him never to do such a thing again.

Trying to imagine how with the passage of time the child can learn to regulate his emotions and his arousal states in the face of the repetition of each of these types of response, we have before us various types of responses that are associated respectively with the development of a secure, avoiding, ambivalent or disorganized attachment.

Safety and security

During his first year of life, the child establishes relationships with his attachment figures that are characterized by frequent moments of emotional attunement, often centered on the sharing of positive and pleasant states of interest, excitement, fun and joy, mediated by an activation of the sympathetic system.

Children who develop a safe attachment to their parents are able to tolerate and regulate high levels of emotional intensity. In the specific example mentioned above, the child's state of arousal (linked to the excitement aroused by the prospect of climbing the table) clashes with the parent's prohibition, which induces an activation of the parasympathetic system and a sense of shame, but which is quickly followed by reparation when the mother takes the child into the garden so that he can use his state of emotional activation in socially more acceptable activities.

The orbital-frontal cortex of this child "learns" that even intense states of arousal (leading to emotional disconnection) can be altered, and that this can help re-establish contact with the parent. In this sense, it is possible to affirm that this type of interactions (connection-disconnection-repair) constitutes one of the ways in which the forms of parent-child communication can facilitate the development of the flexibility of response mediated by the prefrontal cortex.

Avoidance

The child with an avoiding attachment is not so lucky: the parent is emotionally distant, unable to respond adequately to his signals and needs, and his reactions are often characterized by attitudes of neglect or rejection. In these couples the levels of affective attunement are generally very low, and this can negatively affect the development of positive emotions such as interest and excitement; the prohibitions and behaviors of the parent can lead to excessive activation of the parasympathetic system.

Early experiences of the child can have a significant impact on the maturation of his emotional expression skills and on the access of emotions to consciousness: to try to diminish the sense of frustration that results from his interactions with the parent, the child learns to minimize the expression of emotions related to attachment. As adults, these people can pay a very high price in their relationship with themselves, in their emotional relationships, in their relationships with their children; their ability to feel intense emotions, and to perceive the experiences of the mind (their own and others') can be severely reduced, and the result is that their basic emotional needs remain unfulfilled.

On the contrary, they generally believe that their approach to life is entirely adequate, while their private Self remains strongly underdeveloped and inaccessible to consciousness.

Avoiding/distancing adults often seek the help of a psychotherapist as a result of pressure from wives or husbands who have a safe or ambivalent state of mind with respect to attachment, and who can no longer tolerate the coldness and emotional detachment of their partner.

Paradoxically, it is not uncommon that the spouse initially felt attracted to the patient precisely because of his "independence and autonomy: he did not need the others"; for an ambivalent/preoccupied person towards attachment, this meant not having to fear, on the part of the partner, the intrusive and invasive attitudes that had characterized his relationships with his parents.

Over time, however, the ambivalent adult may begin to feel the need for greater emotional intimacy; such a movement towards safer states of mind than attachment occurs much more difficultly in the avoiding partner, not least because the latter is usually perfectly satisfied with the couple's relationship: he is not aware of any problems or suffering, and therefore does not feel the need to change. In these patients, approaches based on rational and logical discussions, which represent for them more natural ways of interacting with others, are generally of limited use; the therapist should rather try to encourage the development of their affective tuning skills, and the activation of processes mediated by the right hemisphere.

By encouraging imagination and other non-verbal processes (for example, inviting him to pay more attention to his body sensations, to listen to music, or even to enroll in a dance school) the therapist can help the patient to discover new ways of seeing himself and the world, and to become more aware of his own and others' emotions and states of mind.

Guided imagination techniques can facilitate direct access to pre-linguistic representations, processes related to the mechanisms of implicit memory and emotional states, with results that many of these patients initially consider "bizarre" and meaningless; however, over time these non-verbal and non-rational processes mediated by the right hemisphere begin to influence their behaviors and their interpersonal interactions.

While within the therapeutic relationship the exchange of communications based on processes of attunement and emotional resonance continues, new models of the Self, and of the Self in relation to others, may progressively emerge, fuelling the search for affective connections; patients may develop greater capacities for integration, more coherent narrative processes, and in general a richer and more complex approach to life.

Ambivalence

In these couples the parent's answers are often confusing and contradictory. Sometimes it tunes in with the child's arousal state; otherwise, the child perceives his or her verbal and nonverbal expressions of anger and disapproval, which can be prolonged over time and generate a harmful sense of humiliation.

Although the limits of its window of tolerance may be relatively wide, in the face of the ambiguous reactions of the parent the child may encounter states of excessive arousal, which are not counterbalanced by an activation of the parasympathetic system; alternatively, parasympathetic hyperstimulation may lead to prolonged states of discouragement and despair.

For these children, separation from the parent means being able to rely solely on their self-regulating abilities, but from their repeated experiences of excessively intense emotional states they have learned that these abilities are insufficient, and therefore paradoxically continue to rely on inconstant and unpredictable figures of attachment. These experiences can lead to an increase in sensitivity, which is manifested mainly in interactions with others and in situations related to losses or separations. In general, there is a maximisation of the expression of emotions related to attachment; according to some authors, the child tries to draw the attention of a distracted and incoherent parent to himself. In individuals who have a history of ambivalent attachment, relationships with parents, dominated by the intrusive emotional states of the adult, may have led to the establishment of a strong sense of vulnerability: they are constantly afraid of "losing contact", with themselves and with others.

To try to meet those around them they can hide behind chameleonic behaviors, which reflect automatic learned responses to adapting their public self to the intrusive attitudes of parents. In the context of psychotherapy, this can manifest itself in an attempt to present oneself as "ideal patients". In the context of the therapeutic relationship these people tend to reproduce patterns of estrangement and rapprochement similar to those that characterized their interactions with parents; while their "private" states of mind slowly become more accessible, the therapist must be able to grasp and exploit the moments of openness that make it possible to establish processes of affective attunement. In order to be able to help these patients, the therapist must be able to receive the non-verbal signals (tones of voice, facial expressions, glances, gestures) that reveal their primary emotional states, and to share these states, rather than simply understand them at a conceptual level.

An important aspect of these mechanisms of tuning and resonance, which involve an "alignment" of the psychobiological states of therapist and patient, is the ability to recognize when the other is trying to create an emotional connection and when instead his attention is directed to the internal processes.

In each of us there are constantly alternating moments when we need to focus on ourselves and phases in which we turn to others; through these oscillations the system of the mind can use internal or external constraints to regulate the flow of its states. These concepts reaffirm the fundamental idea that self-organization is the result of both individual inner processes and dyadic regulatory processes.

It is also thought that the left cerebral hemisphere would have average states of approach, while the right hemisphere would be primarily involved in states of estrangement and withdrawal. The alternation of moments in which the individual is mainly oriented towards the inside or the outside could therefore be at least partly interpreted as the manifestation of cyclical fluctuations in the activities of the two hemispheres.

In the context of the therapeutic relationship, as in general in all emotionally involving relationships, it is inevitable that there will be breaks in the processes of tuning, but if these disconnections are not followed by mechanisms of reparation, may be negative states of shame and humiliation that become serious obstacles to interpersonal communication.

These are not simply unpleasant states, which generate unease and discomfort; the individual can feel sucked into a black hole, into a well of bottomless despair, in which the Self is completely lost.

In order for a repair to take place, it is necessary for the two people involved to realize that a rupture has occurred, and to try to re-tune their states of mind through interactive processes that require the direct participation of both.

The public self tries in every way to avoid these states of shame and humiliation, but even if it continuously explores the social environment to find possibilities of connection it does not always succeed in preventing their activation. In people with avoiding attachment, an imbalance in the activities of sympathetic and parasympathetic systems, linked to inconsistent communications that have characterized their relationships with parents, can make such states particularly difficult to control. The anxiety generated by the emergence of these states at the level of consciousness can induce defensive adaptations. These adaptive defenses of the public self can vary greatly; in some cases they are "primitive" and sterile responses, such as denial or projection of the sense of disconnection on other people.

Some of these individuals may instead adopt more mature and "socially useful" approaches, trying to establish emotional connections with those around them, or sublimating their painful experiences into attempts to help others in their professional lives (for example, teachers who pay special attention to the needs of their students, politicians who draft laws to defend children's rights, or therapists who in their activities place particular emphasis on the need to understand patients and respect their individuality).

In a person with an ambivalent/preoccupied attachment, very different ways of adapting to different social and emotional contexts are therefore possible. In this case, the working environment, characterized by a relative emotional detachment, can favour the development of processes of sublimation, while the intimacy of couple relationships or parent-child relationships can periodically facilitate the activation of an intense sense of "intrusion" or other forms of affective disconnection, which lead to the sudden appearance of the feared states of shame and humiliation.

In an attempt to avoid these painful states, primitive defensive responses associated with anger or fear can be activated, which can be accompanied by perceptual distortions and incorrect interpretations of each other's behaviour; this creates moments of great vulnerability, which can give rise to processes of dyadic dysregulation.

Disorganization

In this case, when the child tries to climb on the table, the mother responds with an explosion of anger that deeply frightens him; it is not only a matter of fear of the consequences of his behaviour: the child fears for his own physical safety. This sudden state of fear, induced by the figure of attachment, corresponds to a conflicting adaptation, characterized by a simultaneous hyperactivation of the sympathetic and parasympathetic systems: the accelerator and the brake are simultaneously crushed. In these forms of attachment, the parent, who often has a history of unprocessed leaks and traumas behind him, provides the child, without necessarily being aware of them, with disorienting and disorganizing responses.

These intense and terrifying experiences of disconnection are not followed by attempts at reparation, and become elements that contribute in an essential way to determine the way in which the child learns to regulate his emotional states and his behavior; the figure of attachment not only does not provide security and comfort, but is in itself a source of confusion and fear.

The presence of unresolved leaks or traumas in parents can lead to the development of disorganized/disoriented attachments, and to dyadic systems that are much more chaotic than those associated with avoiding or ambivalent attachments. In relationships of disorganized attachment, parents' frightened or fearful behaviors are in fact often linked to unprocessed traumas or bereavements: the adult transmits to the child his disturbed processes of self-organization through disordered states and disorienting actions.

These parental behaviours, which can be seen as "biological paradoxes", not only do not provide the child with a sense of security and coherence, but they directly interfere with the development of affective regulation processes and narrative and integrative functions. The result is that the child repeatedly enters chaotic states of mind; from a dynamic point of view, such states can be considered as "strange attractors", dissociated and dysfunctional patterns of neural activations that with the passing of time can become rooted characteristics of the system.

Faced with a patient who has a history of disorganized attachment behind him, the therapist has the difficult task of providing an emotionally safe environment in which the patient can learn to rely on him to modulate his states of mind. Therapeutic relationship and dyadic self-regulation processes are then "internalized", through the creation of a mental model of the Self with the therapist and the progressive acquisition of new and autonomous capacities to regulate emotions. Achieving these new levels of self-organization is often facilitated by integrative processes that allow the development of a deep sense of internal coherence.

Interpersonal relations and emotional regulation

Attachment research provides important tools for understanding how an individual's interpersonal relationships can have profound effects on the maturation of his or her self-regulating abilities. In particular, several studies indicate that the orbital-frontal cortex remains "plastic" throughout our entire existence; in other words, that its developmental possibilities are not exhausted once childhood is over.

Through the exchange of non-verbal signals (looks, facial expressions, tones of voice, gestures) two individuals can communicate and share their states of mind. These interactions contribute directly to determine the nature of their experience at that particular moment; in the context of an attachment relationship, during the child's first years of life they also exert effects on the development of his brain structures that can profoundly influence what will be in the future his mechanisms of regulating emotions.

What emerges from the most recent studies is that interpersonal relationships can provide attachment experiences that allow similar neurophysiological changes even in later stages. In individuals who have suffered severe trauma, such as abuse experiences, deep brain structures may have suffered damage that makes subsequent therapeutic interventions very difficult; however, even in these situations, the principles learned from the study of attachment processes may prove useful in developing approaches that help patients develop greater ability to adapt to stress. In many cases of disorganised attachment and clinical dissociation, for example, therapeutic relationships may favour the maturation of more effective self-regulating processes.

In less serious situations, where the development of deeper brain structures has not been compromised, maladaptive states of mind may have become dominant; in these people the therapy may allow a movement of the system towards more balanced and satisfactory ways of regulating energy flows and information processing processes. Sometimes it is necessary to resort to specific techniques, aimed at modifying particularly deep-rooted patterns of emotional dysregulation. The psychotherapy-patient relationship can provide a sense of proximity and comfort, and an internal mental model of security; throughout our lives these elements of attachment, in the context of a therapy or in the context of other emotionally involving relationships (such as friendships or sentimental relationships), can facilitate further development processes at the level of the orbital-frontal cortex and increase our ability to regulate emotions.

To make it clearer how a psychotherapeutic intervention can help to acquire more flexible self-regulation processes, let's consider the case of a five-year-old girl, who had serious problems controlling her impulses.

The history showed that the girl had serious visual difficulties, which were recognized only when she reached the age of three and a half years; however, even after she had been provided with appropriate glasses, which finally allowed her to focus on objects and individuals, she continued to show, especially at school, impulsive behavior and frequent "emotional explosions". It was evident that the child did not generally look at the people around her in the face, and therefore did not observe the facial expressions of others to "control" how they responded to her behavior. In this case her social reference processes, which are generally already relatively developed by the end of her first year of life, appeared to be clearly insufficient; at school the child seemed to pay no attention to the reactions of teachers and classmates, and this state of "disconnection" gave rise to a picture that could give rise to suspicion of an opposition disorder, or even a basic deficit in social cognitive processes. Direct non-verbal forms of communication play an important role in the mechanisms of attunement and social reference that allow us to perceive the emotional states of others, and that are the basis of the development of the ability to regulate emotions.

During the course of the therapy the child was encouraged to look other people in the face (including the therapist), while her parents and teachers were given essential knowledge about the nature of attachment relationships, social reference processes and the role played by non-verbal communications in the development of mechanisms for regulating emotions; the working hypothesis was that the origin of her social difficulties was to be found in her visual problems, now corrected. After a few months the little patient actually began to look more and more often at the faces of the people she spoke to; playing, she attributed to the dolls feelings and emotions that became an important part of the stories she elaborated with the therapist. With the development of these skills of facial expression perception, social reference and "theory of the mind", I begin to interact with others in a more socially appropriate way. Reflective" dialogues - the fact of talking about feelings, thoughts, memories, beliefs, perceptions - allowed her to develop mental processes that had previously been poorly used.

His ability to regulate emotions seemed to have improved overall: the "explosive" episodes became less intense and frequent, while the manifestations of excessive impulsiveness had decreased significantly. On the whole, it is possible to hypothesize that in all these advances a maturation of its frontal orbital cortex was implied, favoured by new forms of interpersonal interaction.

In theory, this therapeutic approach had allowed the child to learn to use non-verbal signals that in her early years of life, because of her visual difficulties, had tended to ignore; it had allowed her to learn to record basic information about the states of mind and emotions of other people, instead of continuing to live in a situation of social isolation that was for her a source of severe frustration, in which her behavior seemed "impulsive" because it did not take into account the messages and needs of others.

Attachment and integration

The ability to reflect on the history of one's childhood, to conceptualize the mental states of parents and to describe the impact of such experiences on personal development are essential elements of the coherent narratives that these individuals provide in the context of the AAI (adult attachment interview); the ability to reflect on the role of mental states in determining human behavior also profoundly influences their attitude - emotionally available, sensitive and responsive - towards their children. Fonagy and Target have observed that this reflexive function goes beyond a simple capacity for introspection, and has direct effects on the processes of self-organization; we can extend this concept, and say that they also allow the parent to facilitate the development of such organizational functions in the child. Individuals who have a general coherence of their states of mind can more easily establish forms of interpersonal relationships - with their partners, children, friends - that further fuel these integrative reflective processes.

It is thought that the transgenerational transmission of insecure patterns is due to the persistence in adults of states of mind that are inconsistent with attachment; according to the perspectives that consider insecure attachment as a potential risk factor in the development of subsequent problems, understanding the nature of this coherence of mind becomes important for both parents and mental health professionals who are particularly interested in early intervention and preventive measures.

Integration can be seen as a key process, which profoundly influences the trajectory of development paths. In individuals who are unable to establish a sense of internal coherence, adaptive selves with different and incompatible goals and which are a source of anxiety and conflict can coexist; the emotional imbalance of these people can be linked to their inability to diachronically integrate these states of the Self into a unitary and harmonious whole. For example, for an individual who as a child has been repeatedly humiliated attitudes of rejection may continue to have extremely disorganizing effects, even in adolescence and adulthood. The state of the Self, which constantly seeks the consent and approval of others, is faced with the need to emerge and establish itself at school or in the world of work, where the fact of holding a role of power or authority almost inevitably carries the risk of displeasure to other people, and the contrast between these opposing needs can significantly hinder the professional career of these individuals. In all of us there can be conflicts between desires and external reality.

In some cases these desires are part of relatively isolated states of mind, which often remain inaccessible to consciousness but which can give rise to emotional imbalances that manifest themselves with depression, anxiety, uncontrolled anger, feelings of uselessness or strangeness, loss of motivation or difficulty in interpersonal relationships. The studies of Harter and his collaborators indicate that during adolescence the degree of discomfort and malaise is greater the more the individual perceives his roles as "false" and "not authentic"

(Harter et al., 1997). Social contexts that force adaptations mediated by states of the Self that do not correspond to the experiences, mental states and needs of the individual can therefore promote the development of emotional disorders.

In this sense, attachment relationships can act as catalysts as regards, alternatively, the risk of pathologies or psychological resistance, insofar as they facilitate a flow of "non-authentic" or "authentic" states within interpersonal interactions. It can be concluded that insecure forms of attachment confer vulnerability because they do not offer the child interpersonal experiences that fuel integrative processes of self-organization.

Later, relationships with peers or teachers can also play an important role: interactions that influence the states of the Self that emerge in adapting to different social contexts have direct effects on the mental health of the individual.

Although it has been shown that early attachment experiences have a profound impact on the development of social competence and sense of autonomy, it seems clear that subsequent dyadic relationships may continue to influence the maturation of regulatory functions.

Self integration skills, like all functions of the mind, are continuously created by interactions between internal neurophysiological processes and interpersonal relationships; resistance and emotional well-being are fundamental mental processes, which emerge from the integration of energy and information flows within the single mind and between different minds.

Therefore, the lack of integration of significant experiences represents a profound distortion of the system of the Self.

When salient experiences are to be neglected, ignored, underestimated or forgotten, the result is an incoherence of the structure of the Self; different experiences cannot be linked together, and this leads to gaps and fractures within personal history that compromise the complexity and integrity of the Self.

Attachment and reflective function

Children obviously have limitations with regard to their ability to fight or escape and are therefore bound to a relatively small repertoire of actions to modulate agitation and hyperarousal: strong aversion, sucking on parts of their bodies and, above all, dissociation. Through dissociation, the child can enter into a trance-like state and can even ignore excessive or dysphoric inputs, including inner feelings. Perry suggests that repeated failures on the part of the child's caregiver to respond to the child's signs of discomfort organize the child's brain development in the direction of a propensity to quickly tidy up the attack-or-extraction system, and in particular the dissociative component most easily available to the child.

As Stern noted, it seems to be particularly important, in the modulation of the child's emotional regulatory abilities, the attunement of affections between the mother and the children, i.e. the ability of the caregiver figure to intuitively grasp the child's inner states (hunger, agitation, satisfaction and joy) and to respond so as to communicate to the child, "I have understood your message and I can take care of it or I can help you do so".

Stern's research shows that the behavior of about half of mothers agrees with this description in terms of tuning. During these interactions, the heart beats and also other physiological values of mothers and children are in tune.

The tuned behaviour of the caregivers gives the child the idea that behind their behaviour there are internal mental states (feelings, desires, intentions), and that these mental states are such as to make these behaviours understandable, meaningful and predictable. These processes occur, for example, when a caregiver gives meaning to the child's crying and agitation, feeding and verbalizing ("Oh, dear, you are so hungry").

Research in the evolutionary field shows that such interactions not only change the inner state of the child from agitated and dysphoric to calm and satisfied, but also activate a key innate capacity: the ability to understand that mental states are subject to human behavior.

When the caregivers consider their children to be beings with intentions, the child in turn discovers that their behaviour, as well as that of others, is intentional.

Acquiring the ability to grasp social indications and to "read the mind" opens the way to extraordinary human development: the miracle of symbolic representation. There is general agreement that the harmony of the mother-child relationship is a key contribution to the emergence of symbolic thinking. For example, a child placed in front of a visible cliff proceeds over the cliff if the caregiver figure appears quiet, but remains attached if the figure appears anxious. Hobson points out that the central problem, as far as social reference is concerned, is the child's initial appreciation of the distinction between the concrete world as something given and a world in which objects and events can have meanings related to people.

The game and the simulation activity encourage both the understanding of mental states and the development of symbolic processes. Playing with another person, even in an elementary game like the cuckoo, requires an exact synchronization of mental states, affections and time, for fear that the game will stop.

The more the game progresses in the field of simulation, the more the processes of symbolization go on. For example, when a two-year-old boy chooses a stick as a replacement for a gun, he gives the stick a meaning he has chosen himself, which goes hand in hand with his own meaning of thing. When children share their simulated and symbolic meanings with others, they simultaneously keep in mind the two realities, the simulated one and the real one, in sync with a moment-by-moment reading of the mental state of the others who share the simulation.

Contacts with peers and brothers also promote mentalisation and symbolisation. In fact, these contacts can be more decisive in building the childlike ideals and goals of interactions with parents.

This facilitation should not only refer to the growing opportunities for simulated games that peers are able to offer, but also to the multiple, simulated and real, childish roles, which must synchronize in more complex social situations. In this way, the child learns to appreciate the right social indication that indicates the opportunity to be a brother or sister, playmate, rival, child, etc..

Then we have language. The verbalization about the feelings and reasons behind the actions of the child ("Oh, honey, you are so hungry"), are related to the realization of the reflexive function.

But the experience of linguistic use, whether or not it refers to mental states, alerts children to the fact that people receive and produce information communicated by means of verbal and symbolic references. It may be that the critical factor for the development of the child's reflexive function is given by the autonomous reflexive capacity of the figure who looks after him. The ability of the caregiver to read the changes that occur in his mental state at a moment's notice seems to be the foundation of sensitive parenting and the assumption of a secure attachment.

Children who are definitely attached, in turn, can investigate their own and others' minds and demonstrate their ability through additional skills with the tasks of mind theory.

Through play, simulation, interaction with peers, the use of language and intersubjective exchange with sensitive caregivers, the development of the reflexive function feeds the growth of symbolic-autobiographical processes and explicit memory. Explicitly autobiographical memory is also based on a relatively autonomous neurological system.

It, with respect to the implicit and procedural memory that is related to knowing how to do, codifies the information accessible to the consciousness about what things are. This ability to remember autobiographical events and factual knowledge requires the input of the hippocampus and median temporal lobe. Explicit memories, including autobiographical memories, refer to symbolic transformations, as they separate the symbolic representation or meaning of an object or event from the concrete context in which knowledge was acquired.

This knowledge is not expressed through procedures, but through verbal and symbolic references. Explicitly symbolic processes seem to be designed to create coherent patterns, narratives that give meaning to the world, to other people and to ourselves.

Even their most rudimentary level, during the second and third years of life, the symbolic processes and the growing ability to mentalize allow the young child to respond not only to the behavior of others, but also to their conception of beliefs, feelings, attitudes, desires, hopes, knowledge, imagination, simulations, deceptions, projects, intentions of others etc.. For example, the child believes that the caregiver does not respond because he or she is tired.

Or she thinks I'm angry, and she thinks the baby is bad because she wants to beat up her sister or brother. By attributing mental states to themselves and others, children ensure that behaviour becomes meaningful and predictable. As they learn to evaluate the meaning of people's behaviour, they become able to select and activate, from the multiple internal models they have organized on the basis of previous experience, the one best suited to respond adaptively to a particular interpersonal situation.

The effect of this ability to select an internal mediator of behaviour

- even if this process goes beyond an explicit form of awareness
- allows children to transform their whims, impulses and automatic responses to concrete indications into more prolonged and active experiences of decisions and intentionality. This evolution, in turn, puts children in a position to derive a sense of their ability to act and the property of their behaviour. As they gain a sense of intentionality and the ability to act, children also begin to integrate desires, needs, motives, roles and patterns of relationships into a more coherent and continuous sense of themselves and others. This evolution, in turn, prepares the ground for the acquisition of modulating psychological skills that are subject to the regulation of affections, impulse control, self-control and the ability to plan and establish objectives, values and ideals.

Traumas and mourning

The development of the mind can be influenced not only by communication patterns that are established within attachment relationships, but also by specific events: psychological traumas can have a profound impact on the mechanisms of emotional regulation. The secretion of hormones involved in the response to stress can have toxic effects on the maturation of the brain systems involved in self-regulation processes, and in this way early, severe and chronic traumas can compromise the child's ability to respond effectively to subsequent stress.

The nature of the adaptive responses evoked by trauma

- which may be related to the loss of a loved one, to an experience of abuse, to the fact of having witnessed an act of violence
- may differ depending on the stage of development.

In general, traumas and losses can negatively affect the child's expectations for the future, with direct effects on anticipatory models and perspective memory, upset his narrative processes, and interfere with the maturation of mechanisms of self-regulation and integration of the states of the self.

In some cases, particularly deep-rooted forms of dysregulation, generated by a series of combinations of experiential and genetic factors, require the use of drugs, which can facilitate the modulation of the flow of states of the mind through a direct biochemical action at the level of the synaptic connections of the brain, modifying internal constraints of the system. A positive response to drug treatments does not necessarily indicate the presence of "genetically determined" pathologies; for example, drug therapies are often effective in patients with post-traumatic stress disorder. In addition, in studies with laboratory animals experiencing behavioural problems as a result of maternal deprivation, these animals were shown to react positively to the administration of selective serotonin reuptake inhibitors, but relapsed when these drugs were discontinued.

In certain patients, the development of profoundly maladaptive brain structures and self-organizing abilities

- whether related to genetic components, early traumatic experiences or a combination of hereditary and environmental factors

- may require intensive psychotherapeutic and/or pharmacological approaches. In any case, however, it is necessary to keep in mind that the limbic regions (and in particular the orbital-frontal cortex) can remain "plastic", and therefore open to processes of experience
- dependent maturation, during the entire course of our existence, and that any psychotherapeutic interventions can then exploit this potential to facilitate further development of the mind.

Serious traumas that occur in childhood or that induce phenomena of "divided attention" (in which the individual during the traumatic experience enters a kind of trance or focuses his attention on elements of his imagination) can be associated with an inhibition of the processes of explicit memory; the traumatic event is then recorded only at the implicit level, with intense and terrifying memories that can then be reactivated giving rise to images, emotions or automatic behavioral responses whose origin the individual is not able to consciously recognize.

Following the loss of a loved one, especially if it is an attachment figure, the mind is forced to profoundly alter the structure of its internal operating models to adapt to a new painful reality, in which the Self lacks a source of security and comfort.

Experiences of loss can have a strong impact on the development of the mind; the nature and extent of the negative effects may vary depending on the child's age, and the ability of the family environment to meet its attachment needs. In children, as in adults, it can take a long time to manage the suffering generated by a bereavement; a periodic review of the experience can also allow them to use new skills in the processes of elaboration of the loss, which emerge progressively during its development. If the child is not able to change his attachment patterns, these processes of elaboration can be severely hindered or compromised, giving rise to pathological pictures.

Situations of this kind can be favoured by family environments characterized by a general inability to communicate emotionally, which do not allow the child to share his pain with others, or by the presence of conflicting feelings and mental patterns towards the missing person.

Unsolved bereavement or trauma can have profoundly disorganizing effects, of which the individual is often unaware. In essence, this lack of elaboration leads to alterations in the flows of energy and information within the mind; the mind emerges at the interface between neurophysiological processes and interpersonal relationships, and these alterations reflect both on the activities of brain circuits and on the processes of dyadic communication. As we have seen, the presence of unresolved leaks or traumas can dramatically interfere with the individual's ability to establish processes of emotional attunement within attachment relationships, and can therefore also have devastating effects on his children; trying to help these people to recognize and process these traumatic experiences is therefore crucial not only for them, but also for subsequent generations.

In terms of memory, unresolved traumas generate a tendency on the part of the mind to create disorganized states, which are often linked to the sudden and involuntary activation of implicit elements; for example, flashbacks of the traumatic event or mental patterns that refer to a disappeared attachment figure as if this person were still alive.

Such states can significantly interfere with the functions of the mind, in particular with the processes of emotional modulation, flexibility of response and emotional communication, and with its capacity for self-organization. Psychotherapy can allow people with leaks or unprocessed traumas to link these aspects of memory to their past experiences, and thus to understand the causes of their disorders. These reflections must take place in the context of a therapeutic relationship of secure attachment, which allows the patient's mind to go to deeply disordered states and to learn, initially through processes of dyadic regulation, to tolerate them, to reflect on their nature, and finally to modulate them in a more adaptive way. These emotional processes are essentially non-verbal, and probably involve activities mediated mainly by the right hemisphere.

The possibility to consciously reflect on traumatic experience is associated with an activation of explicit memory processes, which allow the consolidation of memories referring to the event in question and their integration within autobiographical narratives.

The development of mentalizing functions and autonomous consciousness also allows the patient to give meaning to the past, to understand and organize the present and to actively plan the future. Individuals who have a history of disorganized attachment can thus get out of the "prison of the present", where they were repeatedly trapped when they had no words to reflect on their uncontrollable and terrifying states of mind.

Emotional resonance: considerations

We all need to establish with others forms of intimate and direct communication, which allow the establishment of states of emotional attunement and mental resonance that help us to organize our internal processes. During our early years, interpersonal relationships characterized by repeated breakdowns in emotional communication, which are not associated with subsequent attempts at reparation and thus evoke states of shame and humiliation, can induce adaptive responses that significantly influence our subjective experiences of ourselves, others and the world, and that create a profound fracture between the public "external" Self and the private inner Self.

The attachment patterns generated by these experiences can have a major impact on the development of our ability to regulate emotions and flexibility of response, on our narrative processes and in general on our attitude towards others.

In some cases, particularly rigid and dysfunctional patterns of self-organization may require psychotherapeutic interventions to try to alter states of emotional dysregulation that are a source of considerable suffering: the "specialized" interpersonal relationships that are established within a psychotherapy provide the patient with a safe environment in which he can begin to explore his present and past experiences. Therapist and patient can enter into states of mental resonance that allow the creation of a dyadic system, in which processes of affective attunement favour the development of more effective regulatory capacities and the movement towards greater complexity. For this to happen, the therapist must be able to perceive the non-verbal signals that are transmitted to him and to respond not only with words, but trying to tune his states of mind with those of the patient, between the primary emotional states, psychobiological, of the two individuals can thus create a direct resonance.

The expression and perception of non-verbal signals are mainly mediated by the right hemisphere; these forms of non-verbal communication, which constitute a fundamental aspect of the therapist-patient relationship and in general of all emotionally involving interpersonal relationships, can therefore be considered as the result of resonance processes between the right hemispheres of the two persons involved.

An active and important role is also played, of course, by the sinister hemispheres of the members of the couple, who are involved in their verbal exchanges and in the logical reflections on the present and past of the patient, and on the experience of the therapy itself. The functions of interpreter of the left hemisphere try to "give meaning" to the experiences of the individual, and to organize his narrative processes. In the dyadic system the flow of states can progressively reach higher levels of complexity as the two individuals manage to establish more coherent interhemispheric resonance states, through tuning processes mediated by verbal communications (from left hemisphere to left hemisphere) and non-verbal communications (from right hemisphere to right hemisphere).

With the emergence over time of different states of the Self, the mind has the difficult task of integrating these relatively autonomous states into a unitary and coherent whole. Psychotherapy can catalyze this fundamental integrative process by facilitating the development of "bilateral" dyadic resonance states, in which the mind of the patient and that of the therapist can be immersed in intense primary emotional states and at the same time focused on reflexive narrative explorations. Passing through these states of cooperative activation, in which processes of affective attunement are combined with reflective dialogues, it happens that the therapeutic relationship can allow the development of more effective capacity to regulate emotions and the emergence of more coherent narratives, and allow the system of the mind to achieve greater complexity, and therefore greater stability.

Psychotherapy is a complex process. The brain can be upset by mental storms generated by complicated interactions between genetic influences and family conflict stories, and both hereditary disorders and adaptations to traumatic experiences can have profound effects on the reality of our subjective lives.

The mind is a complex system, whose activities depend on neuronal connections that are influenced by constitutional and experiential factors, and to help patients achieve more balanced and satisfying levels of self-organization, different therapeutic tools can be useful from time to time, from pharmacological treatments to specific psychotherapeutic techniques. In any case, regardless of the instruments and techniques used, in order to establish an effective therapeutic relationship, the therapist must be deeply committed to understanding and sharing the patient's experiences; he must never forget that interpersonal experiences shape the structures of the brain from which our mind emerges.

For the therapist it can be a difficult task, but also a great privilege, to be able to maintain an objective vision of the emotional needs of the person in front of him, while at the same time allowing his mind to get in tune with that of the other. Through these resonance states, the minds of therapists and patients can unite in a broader dyadic system, which develops specific self-organizing and narrative processes.

In this sense, the therapist-patient relationship reflects in many ways what should be the essence of human relationships: understanding and accepting others for who they are, while trying to fuel further growth and integration.

CHAPTER 6

THERAPY OF REGULATION DISORDERS

Child-parent psychotherapy

This method coincides with the form of intervention developed by Selma Fraiberg, before she applied it to the child-parent program at the University of California, San Francisco. There is a strong and incomprehensible tendency to associate child parent psychotherapy with Selma Fraiberg's activity described in the essay Ghosts in the Children's Room. Fraiberg coined this expression over twenty years ago to refer to the phenomenon that leads the child to be swallowed up by the expectations and unconscious attributions of parents or caregivers. The phrase refers to the fact of being captured in the parents' unresolved psychological conflicts. Fraiberg used this expression as a sort of shorthand abbreviation for the transgenerational transmission of patterns or attachment disorders as well as mental health problems.

The powerful image of ghosts in the children's room has captured the imagination of many clinicians, becoming almost concrete. Ghosts are a way of referring to the role of the newborn in the family, which, among many other things, is the unconscious representative of attachment figures related to the past of parents. When a newborn child acquires this meaning for a parent, it no longer only represents itself, but also someone else, who often remains anonymous. The newborn can thus become the object of negative transference, through which the parent repeats an experience of pain, anger or disappointment not recognized and not exorcised, which he experienced in his earliest relationships.

In other words, the parents' own inner representations of the child and their experience of the newborn's behaviour are distorted by their own past experiences, which, in the new parental context, are now returning. For example, the crying of a newborn baby is not intended as a call for help, but rather as an accusation full of anger, which reprimands the parent because he is not doing things properly and which deserves heavy criticism because of his ineptitude.

In this way, an infant is not just an infant. It is instead perceived as a tyrant, who probably really existed somewhere in the past of the parent who comes back to live through the newborn.

When parents actually experience things this way, they are unlikely to be expansive with an anxious child, and it doesn't matter if others (for example, therapists) try to persuade them to behave in a way that they aren't. Parents are likely to tend to ignore the newborn or respond without feeling guilty, feeling duty-bound or wanting to please the people who are advising them to do so. But none of these alternatives are likely to work in the long term, and even in the short term, because parental conflicts over the newborn will always find another way of expression if the first way of expressing those negative feelings is blocked.

Child-parent psychotherapy has been elaborated as an attempt to correct, mitigate or modify the misunderstandings made by parents and to increase the uninterrupted empathy and pleasure present in the relationship between the newborn and one or more caregivers.

The aspect of child/parent psychotherapy that is acknowledged with less difficulty is the one related to the process aimed at helping parents to understand how intense and pervasive their ambivalence towards the child is, or their real rejection, since this, in the light of the personal negative experiences made by parents, can lead to abuse or negligence towards the newborn. It should be noted that these painful childhood experiences are often removed and are not immediately accessible to the conscious mind of the parent. Alternatively, they can be denied or forgotten altogether, because nothing about what refers to childhood is remembered. Another possibility is that the adult can remember the affective experience and recall it intellectually or cognitively, but is unable to process it affectively; in other words, that there is a form of dissociation from the corresponding feelings. Parents can remember, but without having any feelings for what they remember.

This particular aspect of childparent psychotherapy, namely the effort to connect the present with the past and to seek links between the way in which the first experiences condition current experiences, has led to the therapists' perception as if they were "ghost hunters".

By trying to free the newborn from the past that haunts the parent, child-parent psychotherapy finally aims to help parents come to terms with their child, instead of acting through the child.

In classical child/parent psychotherapy, the child is usually present during the session. In other words, parents are not asked to talk about their past in their absence. His presence strongly contributes to understanding and capturing parental conflicts in all their immediacy and emotional intensity. This immediacy is often more intense when the therapy is practiced at home. The therapeutic process takes place in the natural context of the child's personal space. The therapist tries to create an environment conducive to the re-enactment of images, memories and feelings. At the same time, ongoing interactions between parent and child continue to develop. We are really observing what is happening in these relationships and how this usually tends to happen even when we are present.

It must be said that this kind of activity can also be successfully carried out in the studio, but the house adds a level of immediacy that is valuable as such. Therapeutic activity basically encourages parents to talk about themselves and their baby in their own way

- that is, according to their free associations
- except that in this case free association consists not only of words but also of actions.

This is because while the parents are talking to us, they are also related to the newborn.

When parents talk, we observe their behaviour and the way they act towards the child. At the same time, the child's response to their actions is itself a parallel form of communication. In fact, two different levels of interaction are really occurring; the level of behaviour and the level of verbalisation.

The therapist tries to understand to what extent the things parents are saying about themselves, the child and their first experiences resound in their behaviour towards the child. Sometimes there is a certain contrast between what a parent is saying and what a parent is doing. Clinicians who happen to observe such a contrast will probably try to understand it as an internal conflict within the parent between different perceptions, desires and emotions.

For example, young parents can talk about how, incredibly, they reject their feelings about the child, how they got fat by becoming parents, or even how, sometimes, they would like to kill the child.

However, their behaviour towards their son seems to be invariably empathetic. The significance of such a situation is embarrassing.

Are parents not aware that they are good parents in terms of manifest behaviour? Are they making us realize that empathy is only part of the staging and that they are unconsciously asking not to be disappointed? Probably, parents are asking the therapist to pay attention to what they are saying in the hope of being taken seriously.

Sometimes, what a parent is saying can be so shocking that the therapist takes refuge in what the parent is doing.

The therapist has the responsibility to be in the presence

- with the parents and the child
- of both forms of communication (with words and actions).

In this sense, the psychotherapist of the child-parent relationship needs, in a very precise way, the proverbial third ear of Theodore Reik (1948), an oscillating attention adopted by the therapist to capture and give meaning to the unspoken themes present in the patient's story.

One could say that the therapist also needs a "fourth ear" in order to capture the experience of the child and to ascertain whether or not it agrees with the story and the behavior of the parents.

In other words, the child gives us the overall picture

- which may be consistent or completely different from that offered by the parents
- of how things are going at home.

Consequently, the therapist should devote as much attention to the child as to the words and actions of the parents.

Sometimes, the enormous difficulty imposed by the task of having to divide the attention between a really needy parent and a really needy child is already in itself an important clue to the existence of problems. The therapist, as an emotionally involved participant, is able to perceive the tension, or conflict, that occurs between the needs of each member of the dyad or triad.

Multimodal parent-child psychotherapy

This method of intervention seems to be the one best suited to the needs of families affected by numerous concomitant problems.

In the clinical practice of child mental health, the treatment of these situations requires maximum flexibility, sensitivity to the specific needs of patients and the ability to understand the various problems depending on their importance and severity.

This model relies on an intervention process involving, together with the clinicians, the parents and the child as key partners, in order to understand the problem and try to solve it. The therapist changes roles and techniques depending on the initial problem and the way the situation evolves. The problem we face can be simple in itself, but it can become complex and difficult in the presence of a given family context. Or, it can be just one of many problems that the family is forced to face, including other sources of stress and adverse social and economic circumstances.

Parent-child psychotherapy can be described as the interaction between the family and child system and that of the therapist or therapy team. Optimally, the relationship between these two systems is instructive, satisfactory and constructive for both and results in positive outcomes, or at least the problematic situation improves. In these exchanges, the therapist is ready to modify the interventions, relying on changes and variations in the relationship with the family-child system.

However, if the therapeutic interaction does not lead to mutually adaptive responses to the specific blockage of family problems, the therapy may prove ineffective.

This therapeutic proposal requires the therapist to be highly flexible and capable of employing a certain variety of different techniques. If only one method is adopted to address all these problems, it is unlikely that this will adapt to the actual reality of a specific relationship with the family, the child or the parent-child couple.

When therapists are prepared to employ differentiated interventions, they can apply various strategies to the particular clinical challenge, and take into account factors such as family motivation for change, the specific problem of the child and the concrete constraints imposed by the situation (for example, the journey to be made to reach the therapist, financial limitations). Some of the recommended techniques are useful when the family has too little motivation or resources for prolonged treatment, or when rapid change is needed.

In addition, at different times of the therapeutic relationship, different "theoretical lenses" can be used (for example, family system therapy, psychopathological support during development, behavioural therapy, psychoanalysis), in order to obtain a better understanding of the nature of the problems. These perspectives will inform and guide the interventions.

Multimodal interventions

Not all families respond equally to certain therapy models. For example, some parents with a child who cries "almost all day" may go to the clinician to ask for immediate advice about what they can do to help him. They may feel deeply disappointed if the clinician does not give them helpful advice to make the child cry less.

Therapists who notice their parents' despair can focus their research, from the first session, on the reasons that lead the child to cry like this and, at a later stage, they can indicate how to deal with such a serious challenge (for example, holding the child more often, reducing auditory stimuli, using a dummy).

Once the most painful symptoms have been somehow alleviated or have completely improved, you can shift your attention elsewhere, so as to find out if there are any other disturbances.

The therapist can then become aware of a whole series of problems, such as the feelings of anger or rejection that the parents feel for the child, or the existence of serious situations of stress. If you want to help the child, these problems must eventually be addressed. Alternatively, the process may end at the same time as the parents, after implementing the therapist's initial advice, observe that the child no longer cries as before.

On the contrary, another family with a crying child may not be able to accept the clinical opinion. Parents who have more difficulties with self-esteem or trust in others, and who have been accused by families of not taking proper care of the child, may experience resentment if the therapist initially advises any kind of concrete intervention.

In such a situation, the therapist may find it more useful to propose a reflective model that places first the emphasis on empathy towards the parents and, secondly, towards the child.

The therapist should seek to establish a relationship of trust with the parents, so that they do not feel distrustful of treatment advice.

It is possible to assume that, after these initial therapeutic movements, parents may be receptive to the techniques to be adopted when it comes to calming the child or making him comfortable, and that they serve to prevent further episodes.

A multidisciplinary team (including, for example, family therapists, occupational therapists, speech therapists, doctors, developmental psychologists and psychiatrists) can quickly design multimodal strategies (or a clinician can simply consult with colleagues from other disciplines). When there is a team, clinicians of different backgrounds contribute their specific expertise to the understanding of clinical problems.

Let's take an example:

To give a very general example, on how an dependent relationship can happen, I propose a typical situation, which could be reflected in many homes or families in the world. To make this "story" I will take sample names.

L. is a beautiful child, simple, of those children who never complain, never ask for anything.

If someone approaches smiles, if you ask them something they answer. The important thing is that those who approach, do not require contact from the small. Little L. is a happy 18-month-old boy. His family's very busy. Her parents work, a little like everyone else, but they're really very busy. So busy that they are not there often at home and leave the children to relatives or babysitters. L. has a little sister. Three years. A little bit demanding, active child. Anyone wouldn't realize that L. is, unlike him, hypo-reactive.

At 18 months L. enjoys singing rhymes, songs with parents, dancing or moving. But when L. is left alone, L. only fixes his cars or mechanically backwards and forwards, or makes objects turn or trot repeatedly. Actually, he wasn't actively playing. He used to spend his time. Very sensitive to sounds, L. is frightened by loud cries in a mermaid if hit by loud noises.

The same thing if his little sister, upstairs, approached him to whisper something to his ear. However, if you try to use a normal tone of voice, L. can not divert attention from what he is doing to relate to parents who call him. L., however, if he finally establishes contact, he is very sweet, sociable, affectionate and lively, capable of entertaining social relations. Even if L. relates to others, they have to draw his attention or involve him first-hand, otherwise L. does not deign to enter into communication with someone. He becomes introverted, insecure, stays in his world. He isolates himself and tends to stay in his world and in his activities. Parents, therefore, wonder a little worried, in the future, if this type of character may by chance influence him or give him problems. Of fragility. To be succumbed to other relationships of stronger characters than him. So, we find in a family, a father who anticipates every need and giving everything, giving any kind of protection possible to the child. While the mother tends to encourage the child's assertiveness, even if she is often depressed or inconsistent with herself. Therefore, this basic problem, of having different visions and expressions of the parents, does not impose limits on L.. They have difficulties among themselves that influence the worsening of the problems. L. is up to 30 months old. He understands exactly what he's being told, but he's not a listener. It's discontinuous. Noises, such as crowded restaurants or shopping malls, annoy him but, at the same time, he goes in search of vibrant sounds. L. appears distracted and unattentive. If you try to involve him in the relationship without upsetting his sensitivity, he accepts for a short moment, but then immediately retracts himself by engaging in very simple repetitive behaviors with his toys that keep him away from the world. L. appears really amused only when particular sensory-motor games (running, jumping, turning hard etc.) give him a clearer sense of his place in space, allowing him to organize himself and become aware of his own experience. Often L. tries to examine the environment carefully, but then ends up concentrating on something small placed in front of him. A number of checks have shown that L.'s eyes do not converge very well and that he uses some fragmented visual skills.

The language and symbolic gestures remained very simple, however L. acquired the ability to use language and symbolic play with dolls.

It is particularly sensitive to situations of anxiety, for example, toys that break, dolls that fall and hurt, things that are lost or damaged etc.. L. is able to conduct small conversations on these topics, but anxiety causes him to repeat.

To feel safe, he also uses some compulsive behaviour, including insisting that the door be left open "just a little bit". He is a "fearful dictator" who wants everything to be done as he wants it to be done, so

that he can control the impact of the environment; at the same time, however, he is afraid and does not want others to compete or get angry with him.

Often he cannot tune in if the speaker uses a regular tone of voice but, at the same time, is afraid when listening to high or low tone sounds.

At 30 months he is becoming more and more anxious and inclined to retire to his own world. He doesn't seem particularly fearful or aggressive, but shows that he only feels safe if he follows his own pace; he is cautious about the impact and demands of the outside world. While language and cognitive skills develop regularly, the child cannot pay attention to other people's communications.

L. is hyper-sensitive to some sounds, especially high tones and vibrating sounds, while it is hypo-active to other types of sounds. It is also hyposensitive to movement, and demonstrates poor motor planning ability. It proves to be hypo-reactive to visual stimuli and tends to fix itself and become repetitive. Although there are also affective and interaction difficulties, these have developed according to the problems of hypo-reactivity and activation present since birth.

The child is going through a crucial moment for the development of social interactions and expectations, it would be appropriate to conduct an intensive therapeutic intervention. It was decided to address the difficulties of sensory processing through the sessions of speech therapy and psychomotricity, was also prepared an assessment of visual and motor skills, as well as the responsiveness to auditory stimuli and their processing.

What about anxiety? What can we do when children show anxiety in their developmental age?

CHAPTER 7

Tips: tips for getting out of an emotional addiction

If you are not happy with your relationship, perhaps it is because you are experiencing it from the point of view of addiction. Below are some warning signs that you should be careful about to see if you are sentimentally dependent on your partner.

1. First of all, if your relationship makes you suffer (for example, if it is a source of anxiety and sadness) and, despite this, you are unable to change the situation and interrupt the relationship, you are probably victims of a certain degree of emotional dependence. Relationships are complicated and require commitment and effort, but not suffering.
2. A more concrete signal is not to do any activities outside the couple. Whether it's hobbies, study, a career, friends... If you do everything with your partner, you're likely to be in a dependent relationship.
3. Another characteristic of addiction in the couple is the inability to be alone. You've probably gotten so used to sharing everything with your partner that you don't know what to do when you're alone or you're even overwhelmed by worry: something bad can happen to him or who knows what he's doing.
4. Think or believe that you could not live without that person or that your life would not make sense without him/her, who is

now your whole world. These are typical ideas of an dependent relationship.
5. Jealousy is usually another indication of emotional dependence in the couple, because it is related to insecurity and lack of communication.

Emotional dependence can have many consequences

In some cases the emotional dependence is due to the fact that we have not learned to tolerate the suffering that comes from life and, therefore, we are not able to abandon the partner that hurts us for fear of change or loneliness. The extreme case of this example is that of victims of ill-treatment.

In other cases, however, due to problems of self-esteem, we are dependent on our partner to be valued positively from outside, to be admired and to receive the security that we do not have ourselves.

Regardless of the reason, dependence in the couple is always and in any case a problem for the individual who suffers from it, who must work on himself in order to establish healthy relationships, otherwise expectations, excessive demand for company, jealousy ... will end up deteriorating his relationships.

Do not let your partner occupy your whole being and mind, leaving no room for yourself. To love is not to disappear. (Walter Rice)

1. First of all you have to be honest with yourself and try to understand where addiction comes from. Maybe you are afraid of loneliness because you have never faced it, maybe your self-esteem depends on the flattery of your partner... Think carefully because this is the fundamental pillar to overcome dependence.
2. Reconcile with loneliness. Find spaces where you can be yourself without your partner and, above all, enjoy these moments: you can start doing yoga, join a group of trekkers, enroll in a photography course ... For sure there is something that intrigues you or that you have always wanted to do. The important thing is to know that there is something about you that doesn't depend on your partner.

3. Be aware of your negative thoughts, especially jealousy, fears, etc., and try to be stronger than them. When you realize that you are falling into a spiral of negative thoughts, go for a walk, call someone and talk about it.
4. Talk to your partner. Communication is a fundamental pillar in a report. It is about sharing your experience with your partner to make him/her understand what you are experiencing and the changes you want to adopt. In this way, he will be able to support you and understand you better.

Life is a long road and, when we let go of the reins and abandon our fears and anxiety, we can enjoy all that it has to offer us, especially sentimental relationships, in a much more complete way.

Made in the USA
Middletown, DE
09 May 2023

30317710R00053